SHOOT FIRST

ASK QUESTIONS LATER

JAMES
GUTTMAN

WORLD WRESTLING INSANITY

★ PRESENTS ★

BANG!

SHOOT FIRST...
ASK QUESTIONS LATER

HEAVYWEIGHT

Published by ECW Press
2120 Queen Street East, Suite 200, Toronto, Ontario, Canada M4E 1E2
info@ecwpress.com / 416.694.3348

LIBRARY AND ARCHIVES CANADA CATALOGUING IN PUBLICATION

Guttman, James, 1977–
Shoot first . . . ask questions later / James Guttman.

Title appears on item as: World Wrestling Insanity presents Shoot first . . . ask questions later.

ISBN 978-1-55022-836-6

1. Wrestlers—United States. 2. Wrestling—United States. 3. World Wrestling Entertainment, Inc.
I. Title.

GV1196.A1G88 2008   796.812092'273   C2008-902428-1

Editor: Michael Holmes
Typesetting: Mary Bowness
Printing: Printcrafters

This book is set in Minion and AlternateGothic.

Photos on pages 5, 31, 40, 46, 56, 61, 63, 73, 76, 81, 83, 89, 95, 98, 102, 110, 116, 162, and 165 are courtesy wrealano@aol.com; the photo on page 17 is courtesy Bob Leonard; the photo on page 34 is courtesy Bull Buchanan; the photo on page 35 is courtesy Tom Prichard; and the photos on pages 30 and 152 are courtesy Matt Balk. All other photos are from the collection of ECW Press.

PRINTED AND BOUND IN CANADA

ECW PRESS
ecwpress.com

For Jaimee and Olivia

Table of Contents

Acknowledgments   ix

Foreword   xi

One   **Shoot First . . .**   1

Two   **Bad News, Legends, and Midgets on MySpace**   17

Three   **The Good Ol' Boys**   29

Four   **The Office**   41

Five   **Bloopers, Bleeps, and Ole Anderson**   55

Six   **. . . But You Can't Take
             Pro Wrestling Out of the Wrestler**   71

Seven   **Exceeding Expectations**   85

Eight   **Telemarketer to the Stars**   99

Nine   **Benoit and the Fallout**   113

Ten   **Say it Like it Is, Man**   127

Eleven   **What I'm Trying to Say Now**   141

Twelve   **. . . Questions Later**   155

Thirteen   **Who Would You . . . ?**   163

Acknowledgments

Special thanks to ECW Press, Dr. Tom Prichard, Bull Buchanan, D-Lo Brown, Orlando Jordan, Lisa Moretti, Kevin Kelly, Aaron Wood (who helped with some transcriptions as well), ZAH, Mallory Mahling, Mike Rickard, Canadian Bulldog, Fritz Stephey, Matt Dawgs, all the writers at World Wrestling Insanity, Les Thatcher, Henry Hubbard, Mike Johnson, Dave Scherer, Georgianne Markopoulos, Phil Lowe, Tod Gordon, Jen Hobbs, the subscribers of ClubWWI.com, the readers of WorldWrestlingInsanity.com, the members of the Insanity forums, and everyone else who has had a hand in helping me keep the Insanity going strong for years.

Foreword

Dr. Tom Prichard

The only thing I know for sure is *nothing* is for sure!

I can count my true friends on one hand. I don't trust anybody — I don't really like people in general. In fact, I'm pretty much an a$$hole.

So, why would anybody ask me to write a foreword to their book? You got me . . .

I will tell you this, though. I did not grow up with the Internet; I grew up watching and loving professional wrestling. Wrestling's all I ever wanted to do since I was four years old.

Along the way I lived, loved, and made a lot of mistakes. I've judged, been judged, and formed opinions about people and things I knew little about. When I got to know more about the subject or circumstances, sometimes I changed my opinion, sometimes I didn't.

Well, this book reminds me of that process.

I am the luckiest person in the world. I love what I do. It's only natural to get a little upset or pissed off when people get on a forum or website and completely misrepresent facts or friends of yours. It sucks even worse when it's *you* who's misrepresented or flat out lied about and there's no recourse. It's just out there for the world to read — to believe or disregard.

Too often, people see something on the internet or newspaper and take it as the truth. When James Guttman first called and asked me to do an interview and give some thoughts on his first book, I thought "why not?" I wasn't sure what to expect.

Neither was James.

Now, I think after years of interviewing people in the business James realized that second- and third-hand information had formed his opinion and made him cynical.

You see, a lot of journalists (wrestling and otherwise) will write their story and ask questions later. I gave James my views and he translated them in a pretty accurate way. I can be a jerk — but I can also converse, if you want to converse.

You want respect, you give respect.

And I believe that's the reason for this, James' second book on the insanity known as professional wrestling.

Nobody's perfect. But not everyone in wrestling is "holding so and so back," and not every wrestler refuses to "give up their spot" — which is what some wrestling "journalists," who often have *no* real source whatsoever, want you to believe.

Pro wrestling is a business. A very competitive business. You must have ambition and perseverance and be willing to sacrifice to succeed. If wrestling was easy, everybody would do it. Anybody who has a high-paying, high-profile job can understand the hard work and dedication it takes to stay on top of your game. And when so called "experts" pick you apart without knowing the "story" behind the story? Oh yeah, that's fair . . .

But who said life was fair? Not me! Even though you just read it, I never actually "said" it. Okay, maybe I did — but maybe I didn't!

Anyway, I got to know James over time and even wrote a column for his WWI website. Now he's asked me to write the foreword to his second book. Let me make one thing perfectly clear: I have nothing against the Internet or people on the Internet. Everyone is entitled to their opinion — including the people being opinionated about!

I used to think I was pretty easy going. Then I read a blog about what a prick I am. I thought about it: if I cared, then it would matter. But the thing is, I am a prick. And with good reason. I'd like to think I'm fair, but then I'm sure you would find those who don't think that I am . . .

So why even bother writing this foreword? Well, because James asked me to. I've done a few columns and interviews for the guy through the years. I did them while making a town, getting food, running stop signs, and doing other general, stupid things that I wouldn't want anyone to know about. Of course, I would always ask James to "stop the tape" when I'd order at the drive-thru or be interrupted during the interview. And I would hear "No problem."

And sure enough, during my last WWI interview, James "surprised" me with all my bloopers. You know, the times he "stopped the tape." Funny shit. Real funny shit . . . Not!

James has come to the conclusion that the assumptions he once made were not always the way things really were. Good for him. (I'm sure we'll all change our minds many more times as the years go by.) Nothing is etched in stone. Well, some things are, but most things aren't, so there . . .

I hope you enjoy the musings on the following pages. I would like to leave you with one of my favorite quotes of all time: "Your birth is a mistake you'll spend your whole life trying to correct."

I think that pretty much sums it up. James, if writing this book helps you feel you have somehow "righted" some wrongs, then more power to you, my friend!

Dr. Tom Prichard

CHAPTER ONE

SHOOT FIRST . . .

Everyone thinks they have the wrestling business figured out. We all do. If you watch *Raw* or *Smackdown* or *Impact* as part of you weekly grind, chances are you have ideas on how to fix wrestling — change it, tweak it, and improve it. It's no different than any other pop pastime. Essentially, every hardcore fan of any genre of entertainment can tell you how they'd fix it.

I felt that way about wrestling too. I had it all figured out. I knew all the answers. I had a plan to bring us to the next level. If only Vince McMahon would listen to me, he'd be rolling in gold plated money.

Then I started WorldWrestlingInsanity.com (and later ClubWWI.com) and realized that, well, I didn't know as much as I thought.

That's the irony. You see, when I sat down to write a second book, I wanted it to be very different than my first. After all, once you've done 900 pages on why Triple H killed the Lindbergh baby, there's not too much more to say. And while I still stand by the fact that police found a sledgehammer and bottled water at the crime scene, that's a story for another day.

World Wrestling Insanity (the book, not the website) was a snapshot of one of WWE's creative lows. I stand by what I wrote at the time and meant everything I said. However, once I created the websites dedicated to the book, I never imagined what I would learn.

When WorldWrestlingInsanity.com first went online, the mission was simple. I wanted to bring fans the same humor and commentary I always strived to create, but I also wanted to bring them closer to their favorite stars. Rather than third, fourth, or eighth-hand information, they'd hear their favorite wrestler's thoughts and feelings from their own mouth. No more he said/she said. It was all going to be there, out in the open.

A little over a month after the site went live, Dr. Tom Prichard joined. Dr. Tom was a big part of my first book, and offered a wealth of information. He had been a trainer with WWE, not to mention a World Tag Team Champion. He co-hosted "Byte This." Hell, he did it all. I was truly thrilled to have him on board as a columnist. After all, he had been there and done that, so to speak.

The thing that got me about featuring Tom on the site was everything he noticed. His columns, and his thoughts in general, picked up subtle nuances that I'd never really noticed. It was amazing to see what he was able to see, the missteps he exposed. After all, wrestling was his life.

His columns covered some amazing ground. When Eddie Guerrero died, Tom wrote about the time they spent together in rehab. He spoke from the heart about the passing of his friend, and about the pain that he was feeling. Instead of the grieving process a fan experiences when a star they enjoyed dies, I discovered what a man who knew Guerrero and cared for him felt. It was jarring how this "television death" truly affected someone I spoke to and considered a friend.

Between that and the weekly interviews that followed, everything about the wrestling business began to take on new meaning.

Everything.

My goal from the start was to seek out and interview people I'd watched in the ring. That's it. If you wrestled for one of the major companies, I want to interview you.

And that's about all there is to it.

The reason is simple: every single person who has ever been in the wrestling business has a theory about it. They approach it and think about it differently. They respect certain aspects more than others.

What are they? Well, that's what I really wanted to know.

Every experience is unique. If the *Diff'rent Strokes* theme song taught us anything, it's that "everybody's got a special kind of story."

The other thing I confronted in myself was the way I misunderstood the people behind the characters. Some of the guests I expected to be the strangest or rudest turned out to be the nicest. Some of the ones I thought were going to be really cool . . . were really not.

Here's the kicker, though. What had I been basing my instincts on? TV? Backstage stories and gossip?

How would I know anything? I hadn't been there.

I didn't know these men and women. Honestly, I had no idea what they were like. Just because you wear a cowboy hat on TV doesn't make you a cowboy.

The wrestling business is like high school. Actually, most work environments are like high school. There are rumors and gossip everywhere. Think of any office you've worked in. The new guy's a jerk. The boss is stupid. The copier-repair guy with the eye patch drinks too much. You know the deal.

The difference is: the entire world doesn't know about your office. There aren't websites, newsletters, mobile phone alerts, T-shirts, fan fiction, and action figures dedicated to it. The people gossiping about you and your co-workers actually know you. Their thoughts and opinions are based on personal life experience. Unfortunately, for wrestlers and wrestling, things aren't the same.

Whether it's politics, vendettas, or bad information, many people in the sports entertainment industry wind up getting a bad rap. People may think a performer is the quintessential villain, dead set on destroying the entire business in one fell swoop. In reality? It might be the furthest thing from the truth.

We all have our moments. Sometimes a wrestler happens to have a bad day — and have it in front of the wrong people. Next thing you know, you're that leotard-wearing lunatic who punches the bus driver . . . and the whole world knows it.

Politics? Well, backstage gossip has to begin with someone backstage, right? What's stopping a backstage source from saying, "Undertaker eats his boogers" in an effort to smear his reputation?

There is nothing. That's the sad fact. Whether real or pretend, you're now labeled as a booger-eater and there's little you can do to stop it.

These are just a few things I've picked up, but I'm getting ahead of myself. After all, it took over 100 interviews for me to be able to see these facts as, well, facts. Before I go into detail about what I've learned, it's better if I tell you how I learned it.

So, like I said, my goal when the site was born in October 2005 was to present fans with a weekly interview. I wanted to ask all those questions that everyone was always wondering about.

I chose the name "JG's Radio Free Insanity," taking off on "Radio Free Europe." For a show designed to bring wrestlers to the fans, there was no real criteria besides the fact that the interviewee had to be someone people were familiar with. Out of all the guests we've had, only one hasn't worked for WCW, WWF, or TNA. And because that person is General Skandar Akbar, he doesn't compromise my rule. Because, as any fan of old school World Class Championship Wrestling can tell you, Akbar's freakin' awesome.

So that's where the whole thing came from. For the very first broadcast, I had on Tom Prichard and Charlie Haas. Both men would eventually end up back with WWE, but they were my inaugural episode.

The interview with Charlie was brutal.

Haas was in an airport and waiting to go to Italy with his wife, Jackie. He was distracted and didn't have much time. If the same situation occurred now, I would just postpone the whole thing. Since I was new to all this, I wasn't prepared for that kind of situation; my mindset was it's now or never. Grab guests when you can, otherwise they disappear into the ether. I don't know. I'm pretty sure that was my thought process at the time.

As the weeks went by, I interacted with many different personalities and started to learn how to make my interviews work best. In September 2006, I created ClubWWI.com to house the archives of past shows and present full, uncut interviews with each week's guest. When the Club first opened up, we were close to a year into

"Radio Free Insanity," so new members immediately had access to hundreds of hours of audio.

Like I said, the basic premise behind each of the shoots is to present fans the stars as they really are. The public's perception of wrestlers is often misinformed. It can be due to any number of factors, but one of which is often the performer's desire, their intention, to control the way they are perceived. The first time I truly understood this was the day I interviewed Kevin Nash.

Kevin lives with the stigma of being the man who many people feel "killed" WCW. Apparently, he hates wrestling companies. . . . He likes to see them crushed beneath his giant boots as he devours TV time for dinner. To some, Nash represents everything wrong with the wrestling business. In their eyes, he's horrible, mean, nasty — the kind of guy who should be sent to live alone on an island, where he can't hurt anyone.

In reality, he's one of the few people in wrestling who called me back for his interview at the exact time he said he would.

Kevin Nash leads the nWo

It's stuff like that you don't hear about. I can't tell you how often I've been told, "Yeah. I'll give you a ring tomorrow. We'll do it then." A week later, when I finally track them down, it's "Tomorrow. I'll ring you tomorrow." The game usually goes on for a few weeks. I've had some stars play this way for a year before we actually recorded. Greg Valentine holds the record. He agreed to be interviewed in December 2005. I finally recorded him in April 2008.

Big Daddy Cool wasn't like that. He told me he'd call at 2:45 p.m. the next day and just as the clock hit a quarter to three, my phone rang. It was the first surprise in what would be an interview full of revelations.

As I mentioned, many stars have a negative image, and Kevin's reputation is legendary. After all, he's turned his backstage "evil" into a gimmick. Upon his TNA debut, he took the microphone and told everyone in the company that he was devoted to making them so miserable they'd quit. It was more than enough to annoy the fans who felt that this went beyond a role he was scripted to play. To them, it was the truth, delivered by someone capable of following through.

I asked him about it. Considering how much he plays it up, does he feel that fans don't know the real Kevin Nash? That they only know the most negative things?

"God, I hope so," he said.

With that, everything began to make sense. It's an industry full of insanity, where many embrace rumors because they're often more entertaining the truth. It's a tried and true principle of entertainment in general: if they're talking about you, then they're thinking about you. So many of wrestling's most charismatic stars have embraced this principle; they don't want to squash negative stories. They actually embrace them, as little more than another layer to the character they're trying to sell.

Few do this better than Kevin Nash.

As the interview went on, Kevin addressed so much that surprised me. You see, just because he embraces the negative stories, it doesn't mean he's happy about all of them. He wasn't too happy, for example, about people blaming him for the demise of WCW. He brought up how there have been books written attributing its death to him, and how the writers who did so weren't seeing the big picture. After all, the real death of WCW — in Kev's eyes — was the unwillingness of TNT to continue airing the show after Time Warner merged with AOL. Still, it's didn't stop him from sarcastically taking the blame.

"You know what? Every night I toss and turn because I killed WCW. I haven't slept since."

Although he said it in the traditional Nash too-cool-for-school way, the statement went much deeper. He seemed genuinely fed up with hearing about it. After all, anyone who listened to the entire interview could plainly hear how much he loved working for World Championship Wrestling. In fact, any fan knows that Kevin has never found a new home that welcomed him the way WCW did. He was the king of that company and, if it were still around today, he'd still be king. He truly seemed to enjoy being there each week.

"It was a party too, man. And the party carried on after. I loved going to work on Monday."

So, while people have said that Kevin Nash's political games killed WCW for years, few have ever looked at it from his point of view. Even if you blame him for the company's demise, you need to realize that it was still something he really cared about: hey, he was being paid huge money to party each and every week. To say that anyone would destroy that, on purpose, borders on the insane. Doesn't it?

But that doesn't mean he didn't play a part in *accidentally* killing WCW. There was clearly no malice or forethought. In fact, hearing him talk about his WCW run was like listening to a 40-year-old former frat boy tell stories of mid-'80s keg stands. It was obvious he missed the fun.

When it comes to my interview style, I guess you can say there are certain ways I approach things. I'll talk about this throughout the book. Something I should make clear right away, however, is that I always try to make things easy-going, comfortable, and conversational. If a performer says something that reminds me of something I've always wanted to know, I'll bring it up and let things digress. I do pre-show research, but I don't make lists of questions. I've found this makes the interview flow better.

But it also means I run the risk of asking something insulting, unintentionally. . . . And that's what I did with Nash.

"The timing of losing the TV and the AOL buy-out and all that happened when the company was hitting a creative low," I said. "Do you think that a lot of fans only watch the product and say, 'Well, they went out of business because the shows were so bad'?"

As soon as the words escaped my mouth, I realized what had happened. Sure, the shows were bad. We all know that. Well, maybe not all of us. After all, there were a number of people who helped write those bad shows. I'm sure they liked them. One of those people was — you guessed it — Kevin Nash.

After a brief pause, he responded.

"The show was bad. . . . Yeah, the show . . . Was it a creative down . . . How was it a creative down point?"

Alright, so I'd made a huge mistake. It actually yanked me back into reality of the situation. This wasn't just me and a buddy talking rasslin'. . . . This was Diesel.

But the thing with Kevin is that he's just so easy to talk to. It didn't take a rocket scientist to see why he'd gone so far in the industry. There was a real charm about him — you can see why a promoter might say, "Here. Take the show and do what you will with it. You're a super guy!"

The final moments of that interview are still among my favorites of any I've ever done. It was close to Christmas, and I closed things out by plugging all the action figures Kevin had on sale for the holidays. He started to name all the dolls he had coming out. I couldn't help but throw in a figure from his past — part of the most disturbing series of toys ever made.

"And if you have Kevin's vibrating WCW figure, you can . . ."

Nash laughed and told the listeners, "Give that one to Mom!"

Awesome.

Even without the closing line, I was impressed with Kevin from the very minute he called me back. Kevin Nash . . . well, he exceeded expectations. That happens rarely.

Larry Zbyszko

Larry Zbyszko was the same way. As I write this, I still have his voicemail saved on my cell. He blew my mind.

Larry was a guy I watched and loved as a kid. I remember discovering him in the AWA and laughing as he called people "jerks." He didn't just say it. He spit it out the same way you'd say a curse word. He was boisterous, loud, and claimed to live in the fictitious LarryLand. He was like Jim Belushi, if Jim Belushi could kick your ass. The AWA champ was the man. Years later, as a WCW wrestler and announcer, he still got a big pop every time he came into the building.

Interviewing Larry Zbyszko was a trip. It was everything I thought it would be, and more.

Those who listen to the interview might not realize it, but Larry was at a casino when I called. Not only that, but we also were on the phone for quite a while before the interview began. The reason? A raffle.

It's something I'll never forget. Larry had made some time to head outside and talk, but when I called, he had to wait for the winner of a raffle he had entered to be announced. I waited with him.

The people were loud as hell. (What do you expect? It *was* a casino.) As we all sat with baited breath, they called out the name of the first winner. It wasn't the Living Legend; it was some woman. Larry booed.

He asked me to wait, though, because if she had left, they'd call another number. So we waited. People were yelling. Zbyszko told me a bit more about the raffle, some distracted small talk, until it became apparent the winner wasn't there.

So the called the next name. It wasn't Zbyszko. Once again, Larry booed.

At this point, the odds were the prize would be claimed, so Zbyszko headed outside to do the shoot. He was at the door when he heard them announcing another name. Apparently the second winner wasn't around either.

When they called out the third name, Larry started to yell. He said he had to get back inside because it sounded like they called his name. Apparently he had won the big prize. Happy days.

Not so fast. After reaching the stage area, he heard the winning name more clearly. He explained that his real name is "Larry Whistler," while the winner's was "Weesler." So once again, there was disappointment, and after a few more minutes, someone finally claimed the money.

Larry booed, called the woman something better left unprinted, and said, "Okay, James. Let's do this."

Zbyszko dealt in plain talk. He didn't dance around or play games. He said what he meant and that was it. Everything about him was very matter of fact. Case in point: my question about announcing for WCW *Nitro* during its dying days. Here I was, with one of those deep questions about how he felt having to promote a product that was dying. He couldn't have made it any easier to understand: "God. I wanted to kill myself!"

Then, he shot on the McMahon family and blamed the invention of the clothesline on a lack of wrestling ability. He didn't seem bothered by small details. In a nutshell, Larry Zbyszko seemed like the kind of guy you'd like to have sitting at your blackjack table. In every sense of the word, he lived up to who he was on TV.

The whole setting of the interview once again led to the show's closing moment — but I'm not sure many people got it. As things wound down, I gave Zbyszko a chance to speak to his fans, and thanked him for his time.

"Hey, James! I'm going back into LarryLand to gamble!"

He was serious. He had renamed the casino LarryLand. The guy was the real deal.

Aside from giving fans a chance to hear from performers about themselves, I want to give wrestlers the chance to express their

Tito Santana

opinions about the people they've worked with. Sometimes what they say can be shocking. And sometimes this kind of thing comes out of the last person you'd ever expect it from. . . . I never would have thought Tito Santana would shock me. But he did. Sure, there have been other shocking statements from guests.

"There's a lot of guys who understand their role. But then there's a lot of guys, these smaller, younger guys, that read about how great they look, you know, because they can do all these acrobatic moves and get this big, you know, ego. And they get this mindset, 'Well, I should be pushed more.' Well, if you think you should be getting pushed more, go out there, get bigger so you can beat these bigger guys. Bottom line? Work out more. Sad thing to say, but do steroids, put on 20 pounds to go out there and make it look like you could beat the guy. Because the bottom line is that 90% of people who watch wrestling look at the two people before the match starts and say, 'That guy should kill that guy.'"
— **Disco Inferno**

Seriously. Glenn Gilberti said that. On air.

Okay, maybe you expect controversy from a guy like Disco, but not from El Matador, right? For those who don't know who Tito Santana is for some insane reason — in the 1980s, he was as much a part of WWF as the ringposts. He was the go-to wrestler for a solid match, and he was the quintessential good guy. Immortalized in cartoon form, Santana was always ready with a smile and an "Arriba!"

Tito also made good in the long term. An example of a wrestler who was able to transition back to normal, everyday life well, he is now a Spanish teacher in New Jersey. Santana occasionally does shows or autograph signings, but off the clock, he's Merced Solis.

Tito addressed something that I don't believe I'd ever heard discussed before. He spoke about the time in the '90s, just prior to Bret Hart's WWF title reign.

> "I think, at the time, they were thinking about expanding the World Wrestling Federation to Mexico and to parts of South America. And I think they were even considering me for the World title at one point if they had gone in that direction. Within the next two years, the direction changed, and they ended up expanding Canada instead of Mexico and South America. And that's why they ended up going with Bret Hart, from what I see . . . I'm just trying to read into what I saw. Nothing was told to me, but I'm not stupid. I could see what was going on."

Santana says that although they tried to play it off like a last minute decision, he knew the process had started months earlier. Hart was the World Champion and McMahonifest Destiny moved north rather than south.

> "I had nothing to complain about. I would have liked to have been the World Champion. . . . But, and I hate to say this, Bret Hart's divorced. I'm still married. Who's ahead? I've still got my family. At the end of his career, God bless him, he was a World Champion. The family to me was always very, very important."

Uh? Whoa . . . I didn't see that coming.

A little below the belt? Yup. Strangely, though, the more I heard about Bret "The Hitman" Hart, the more I could see why there might be some animosity. He sounded like someone who may have taken things a wee bit too, um, seriously.

Tito wasn't the only one who talked to me about Bret in surprising ways. Growing up, I watched Hart face off against "The Mountie" Jacques Rougeau. They had a run of matches together, both on television and at house shows. One of the most memorable

Jacques Rougeau, Lance Storm, and Bret Hart

was Bret's loss to Jacques just days before the Royal Rumble. Rougeau won the title and would later drop it to Roddy Piper. The strange thing, though? They kept saying that Bret had a fever on the day he lost it. To me, the whole thing seemed kind of lame. I mean, come on . . . a fever? I've seen guys wrestle with casts and neck braces.

Take an Advil and wrestle, Hitman!

But to my mind, that wasn't the only thing linking the two Canadians. Somewhere, in the back of my mind, I recalled a story I read about Hart pinning the Mountie in three seconds — a wrestling record. The story went that Bret rolled him up just as the bell rang and the referee counted three. For over 15 years, I thought this was a fact.

When I asked Jacques about it during his interview, the floodgates opened.

"Bret was a headache. Bret was a real headache in the business. I think what happened with Shawn Michaels in Montreal — I don't know if you heard about it in the States — when Bret didn't want to give the belt to Shawn Michaels. That's something that I feel sorry for Bret that he never understood. Bret Hart became Bret Hart because the Fabulous Rougeau Brothers put him over with Jim "The Anvil" Neidhart every night. And the other teams that worked so hard to create him. He wasn't a true champion because he was a great wrestler or winner. He was a true champion because all the other boys helped him get his status. I think that's one thing in life that he never understood. Maybe that's why Hulk never wanted to work with him or put him over. Because he was worried about what he looked like, if he lost. I remember him losing to me his Intercontinental Title. . . . He had to make Vince, he made Vince announce just before his match, before we started the match, that, 'Although the doctor suggested that Bret should not wrestle tonight because of pneumonia, he still wants to go in the ring tonight and defend his title.' So he's taking all the credibility away from me winning the belt because he was sick. He never understood that we're the guys who created him and made him somebody. Some other people told me about this three-second win. Power to him if everyone believes that today."

Well. No more mentions of a three-second match from me.

In the same interview, Jacques spoke highly of Hulk Hogan, shooting down any thought that he might be bitter. After all, Hogan had even let Rougeau pin him in Montreal. It's almost unheard of and, according to Jacques, it was all the Hulkster's idea. Few would have expected to hear that, but if you look at the general philosophies both guys had, it's actually quite easy to understand.

What really separates someone like Bret Hart from Hulk Hogan is this: Hogan was interested in making money; Bret was interested in making history. When people were throwing money at Hulk, his opponents were able to grab some too. When Bret was making history, his opponents were listed as losers.

On top of that, Hulk's entire gimmick was based on making his opponents look good . . . at least for 15 seconds. No matter how crappy you were. No matter how many matches you lost. You were guaranteed to get at least a few punches in on Hogan. After all, how else could he do his Hulking-Up/seizure thing?

Bret didn't Hart-Up. He just outwrestled you and made you look ridiculous. In the end, he raised his arm and walked up the aisle. And maybe, for some reason, that never went over well with opponents who'd just made him look good. . . .

And although there have been others who've had harsh things to say about the Hitman, few have spoken as plainly as Allen Coage. When I asked Bad News Brown about his 1988 program with The Excellence of Execution, he had this to say:

"The first time I met Bret was in 1980 in Japan. . . . His father, Stu Hart, was the one who brought me up here to Canada. . . . I knew Bret was a prima donna and a crybaby, but I figured if we could put up some good matches that we did in Calgary, you know, we had a chance to make some money. With me, I've always said I was in this for the bankbook; I'm in this for the money. But some people are in there to build up their own ego, or, you know . . . that was his problem. He always believed his own BS. He didn't realize. Because I told him one day, I said, 'Look, man, you're not the World Champ. You're the promoter's champ. Okay? So just be happy that you're making money.' But he was never satisfied with that. It was always that he had to be number one, you know."

It was an honor to speak with Bad News. As a fan of his for decades, I was thrilled that I had the chance to have him on.

Less than three months later, he passed away at the age of 63.

CHAPTER TWO

BAD NEWS, LEGENDS, AND MIDGETS ON MYSPACE

I'll remember interviewing Allen Coage for a number of reasons; for starters, as a New Yorker, I grew up with Bad News Brown in WWF.

Sure, it wasn't the height of Bad News Mania. The lucky fans of Calgary got to see his real grade-A material with the likes of Dynamite Kid and Owen Hart. What I got, though, was the wild-eyed ghetto blaster from Harlem. And while fans across the country appreciated Brown, it was New Yorkers who really felt the gimmick spoke to them.

Bad News Brown

After all, this was our badass "hometown" hero. When he countered Jake the Snake's snake with his own animal aggressor — New York City sewer rats — we all cheered.

Woo-hoo! Those are OUR rats!

Before it was customary for heels to batter authority figures, Allen turned heads by being one of the only guys — if not the only guy — to physically assault then-WWF president Jack Tunney as part of a TV storyline. Making this even better, he accused Jack of getting "special favors" from Miss Elizabeth, and then did his crazy bug-eyes thing.

The "assault" — although nothing more than a jerk of Tunney's collar — left an impression that was stronger than any chairshot you see today. The simplicity of it all, the perfection with which Coage played the villainous Bad News, made it work.

Complete honesty here: on the day I was supposed to interview Allen Coage, I wasn't in the mood. It was near the end of the year, and I had a laundry list of things I needed to get done and no time. I could barely find the time to brush my hair, much less interview Bad News. The fact that it was Bad News Brown is probably the only reason I didn't postpone the interview.

Today, I'm grateful I didn't. Allen Coage was tremendous. When it came to shooting, Bad News was straighter than the best of them. He simply didn't BS. He spoke his mind and laid everything on the line. He also dealt with the business in a way that, at that point, I hadn't experienced.

Allen didn't care if you beat him. He didn't care how many times a night you beat him. He would put over anyone at any time — on one condition: you had to pay him.

As I mentioned earlier, he was open about doing what he did for the money. Sure, he loved wrestling, and excelled at it, but Bad News didn't care about how he looked in defeat. He wasn't concerned about spots or card placement. All he wanted to do was go out there, put on a good match, and collect his money.

Because of this, he was involved in angles that others might have turned down. One such example came at *WrestleMania VI*. Feuding with Roddy Piper, Allen undertook the strange task of wrestling him on the most important pay-per-view of the year. The bizarre note? Hot Rod was painted half black.

Back then, Piper would do interviews and speak normally — when showing his white side. Then he'd turn to his black side, the side greasepainted, and talk jive. It was "cutting edge" television, yeah. But it's also completely batshit insane when you examine it in hindsight. Knowing how crazy the P.C. police are today, the whole angle only serves to remind me of how old I am. Could you imagine a half-black Rowdy Roddy Piper on today's cable networks? People would lose their minds. And send in Al Sharpton to shoot him.

At the end of the '80s, they cheered.

When I asked Coage about the angle, I expected the stock wrestler response. I figured he'd say, "Roddy was a great mind. We felt this would be a natural way to draw on the heat I got by being the mean man from Harlem. The idea was that he was trying to get under my skin."

I say that, because that's what happens when you ask wrestlers about ill-conceived angles. When you ask someone involved with something like this to explain it, they almost inevitably respond by repeating the specifics of the angle back to you.

They explain why it was supposed to work . . .

"I used that racial slur so the people in the audience would get mad because racial slurs are bad."

Then they tell you that people liked it.

"People still ask me about that today. They talk about how it was ahead of its time."

So yeah, I expected to hear the same old, same old when I asked Bad News about the Piper black/white silliness.

I was, shall we say, wrong.

Roddy Piper

"I knew where Piper was coming from because I knew him before I worked with him in the WWF. That's his mindset. The guy's a total bigot. I figured he wanted to do it, so go ahead and do it. I figured some of the brothers would get ahold of him and beat the crap out of him."

If I was drinking a glass of water at the time, I would have done a Jerry Lewis spit take. Talk about no-spin. Bad News didn't mess around.

Allen Coage spoke openly about his time in the WWF, and in hindsight he wasn't too happy. According to Bad News, he was promised many things by the company, only to see few, if any, materialize. He talked of being guaranteed a World Title run, and the prospect of being the first black World Champion.

Wrestling fans know that never happened. It affected Coage and, his wife, observing the toll WWF life was taking on him, urged him to leave. At 63, he was still ready to do his thing; Bad News was still going strong.

All in all, Allen Coage lived up to the hype, and then some. As a kid, if you asked me to pick a wrestler who probably wouldn't BS you in real life, simply based on their TV character, I'd have picked Bad News Brown. His tough exterior told you that he didn't mince words or sugarcoat opinions.

Happily, I grew up to find out that was true. By the end of the interview, I had a new respect for Bad News Brown.

When we were done, I stopped the recorder and spoke to Allen about when his interview would go up. I told him I would be happy to help promote any upcoming shows or events he might have (a courtesy I extend to all guests). But he had another, very different request.

"Actually, did you mention that you had written a book?"

I did. During the interview, I brought up the book *World Wrestling Insanity* when making a point on WWE. Bad News remembered and asked if I could send him a copy. I had it out the next day.

That was truly a remarkable moment for me. As I said, Bad News Brown was a guy I used to see at Madison Square Garden. Here he was many years later . . . wanting to read my book after our interview. It was a huge honor for me.

It was as if He-Man, Lion-O from the *Thundercats*, and the 1986 Mets wanted to read my book. Bad News Brown was that big of a part of my childhood.

I hadn't had a chance to call Allen back to find out what he thought about the book when I heard he had died.

You can imagine what a shock it was for me. He sounded great during the interview.

As I said at the time (and I'll say again here), I wasn't Bad News Brown's best friend. There are tons of people out there who knew him much better. The thing that got me was that I had the chance to interview him just before he passed away. I count my blessings. Had I not kept that appointment, I may have never gotten to know Allen Coage — the man behind the Bad News Brown character.

I'm often asked how I decide who to invite on the show. Sometimes guests are topical. Others are names from the past with big stories to tell. People like that usually come my way after I spend time reading through lists of past WWF and WCW employees: it isn't always fun.

Typically, I'll study lists of names who worked in the '80s or '90s, looking to find someone who hasn't been interviewed over-and-over again, and then I try to convince them to come on board. Reading through the names can be pretty depressing, though. . . .

Rick Rude. Curt Hennig. Kerry Von Erich. Big Bossman. Andre the Giant. Brian Pillman. Davey Boy Smith.

There are so many wrestlers who've passed away, far too early. And no, this isn't a big statement about deaths in wrestling. This is a statement about people I watched when I was a kid, men and women I'll never get the chance to interview.

I'm not being glib; I'm 100% serious. When I get the chance to talk one on one with someone in the wrestling industry, I feel like I get to know them better. I understand them on a different level, and give the listeners a chance to do the same, and I learn the way they think that wrestling should work. It gives me a deeper appreciation for the person who portrayed the character I had grown to know.

In the case of some of my all-time favorites, that can't happen. I didn't get to shoot with Brian Pillman about threatening to pee in ECW's ring; I didn't get to ask Owen Hart about his win over Bret at *WrestleMania*. I didn't get to ask Yokozuna about playing heel on the U.S.S. *Intrepid*.

I did, however, get to ask Bad News Brown about his match against the half-black Roddy Piper. That's something I can be proud of. I got to share Allen Coage's last interview, and now, when some-one asks, I can tell them what a straight-up guy Bad News truly was.

I also had the pleasure of shooting with Dewey "The Missing Link" Robertson just before he passed away. Link was in a different boat.

Older than Allen, and in failing health, Dewey had set out to market a book he'd just written and warn young people on the dangers of drugs.

Back in the day, though, Missing Link was insane. Everyone remembers the first time they saw him.

Why? Because he was freaky. Imagine a jacked guy with a green head and poofy hair . . . that was the Missing Link.

He spent time working many different territories, including the WWF, where he was managed by Bobby Heenan. But ultimately, Dewey Robertson was well known wherever he went. There are probably still fans in the WCCW area who have nightmares about Link head-butting them in the middle of the night.

Dewey Robertson as The Missing Link

One of the hardest things about interviewing Dewey was trying to get over the shock. It blew my mind: the Missing Link was talking. It's like when I interviewed The Ugandan Giant, Kamala (a.k.a. Jim Harris). Most listeners were so taken aback hearing the face-painted island monster speaking with a thick southern accent that they didn't pay attention to what he was saying. When you haven't heard a wrestler speak for 20 years, and then, suddenly, he's engaging in a one-hour discussion, it knocks you for a loop. Actually, it works both ways. Other guests in Link's boat have talked about it. . . .

"I get kinda nervous because I haven't talked as Nick Dinsmore since early 2004, and sometimes, doing an interview as Nick Dinsmore, I forget what I'm supposed to say and not just make funny faces and lick my lips."
— **Nick "Eugene" Dinsmore**

In the case of the Link, he had a strong message, and he spent his final years really trying to make a difference. He spoke at churches and schools to try to keep youth away from drugs. It's one thing to atone for your sins when you get older — it's another to try to help others avoid the same mistakes you've made. That's what the legendary Link did.

It's strange for me to refer to wrestlers I grew up watching as "legends." It seems like just yesterday that some of them were in the ring. Actually, for some, like Terry Funk, it *was* just yesterday.

I've had a chance to talk to a ton of legends on ClubWWI.com. Harley Race, Dory Funk Jr., Bruno Sammartino, Terry Funk, Nick Bockwinkel, The Valiants, and others have all joined me for shoots; and in each instance, it was mind-blowing for me to think about who I was speaking to.

That's something that many people don't get about WWE's Hall of Fame. The Hall is a hot button topic, and it's come up countless times during interviews. The reason is simple: how can a Hall of Fame, where induction is largely based on politics, or the regional location of the annual ceremony, be a true Hall of Fame? How can it honor Bob Orton, but not Bruno Sammartino? Sure, okay, yeah, Bob was a great technical wrestler . . . but Bruno was — I don't know — champion for 11 years!

It seems like a no-brainer, right?

Sammartino, during his interview, didn't seem to be bothered by the situation. He just didn't want anything to do with it.

"If you want to go to this Hall of Fame to watch all of this . . . It's a joke! In my opinion, and people don't understand this, it's a gimmick for McMahon to make even more money. What they do, they have this Hall of Fame thing. They make DVDs out of it. They do the thing when *WrestleMania* is on, the day before or whatever, all this publicity . . . Then he's in 120 or so markets around the world. The Hall of Fame is inducting . . . blah, blah. They sell it. They sell it. They make money. But in my opinion, it's all a scam. It's not a legitimate Hall of Fame."

Everything Bruno said was true. It's not a true Hall of Fame. There's no building. There's no review committee. There are no criteria, just whomever WWE decides to honor. That's it.

Politics and geography.

But here's the thing. Why is that so bad? I mean, sure, it's bad if you call it the true "Hall of Fame," but as the years go by I've realized that we're all hung up on the name. It's the whole reason people freak out so much.

You see, wrestlers and promotions both fall into the same trap. Sometimes they try so hard to exaggerate the importance of a gimmick that it becomes transparent and takes away the spotlight from what truly makes it special.

Stop for a second and imagine if it was called "WWE's Legendary Honors" or "WWE Legends Appreciation." If that were the case, would we all be debating how it is that Randy Savage isn't in, but George Steele, who was pounded by him in countless matches, is? When it's simply seen as an honoring ceremony, there's no "he's in/he's out" mentality.

Every legend deserves to be honored. But that takes the debate out of the whole thing.

We should be able to sit back and accept the night for what it is: an evening to watch stars from the past feel honored for what they've done. For one night, WWE legends are the stars and today's wrestlers became fans along with the rest of us.

That's the issue for me. While I'm with Bruno on the gimmick that the Hall truly is, I can't help but think there's something nice about seeing a performer from yesterday break down in tears.

And to see today's wrestlers marking out for them.

Many members of the Hall of Fame have been on ClubWWI.com. Each time out, they say the same thing: the Hall was an honor that they'll always remember. Guys like Nikolai Volkoff, Jimmy Hart, The Iron Sheik, Bobby Heenan, and Tito Santana have all spoke to me about how proud they were to be, well, honored.

Simply put, that's what I most like about WWE's annual spectacular. It honors men and women for the hard work and dedication they've shown. I can't agree more with that sentiment. The wrestling business is unique in that many of its pioneers go on to train younger stars. Imagine if Oscar-winning actors routinely retired and opened acting schools. It doesn't happen. In wrestling, it does.

Harley Race springs to mind here. I spoke to Harley for quite a while. In the end, his interview clocked in at an hour and ten minutes. That's not because he was long-winded or because he droned on. It's because, to me, the opportunity to speak to Race was just overwhelming. And I'd talk to him for as long as he wanted to talk to me. What he's done for this industry is unparalleled. What he continues to do is as well.

Harley runs a wrestling school in Missouri and operates World League Wrestling. In essence, Race wrestled until he couldn't anymore. Then he managed until he couldn't anymore. Now he's training the stars of tomorrow until the day comes when he can no longer do that. You can't get any more dedicated to wrestling. But Harley must be unique, right?

Wrong.

How about Dory Funk Jr.? His story is nearly identical — right down to my interview with him. Funk and I spoke for 65 minutes, and it was for all the same reasons. One of the most successful grapplers ever, at the time I spoke with him, Dory was running his own wrestling school and producing "Bang! TV," an internet-based show that featured the stars of his school and established wrestlers from WWE and TNA.

Oh, and did I mention that at 67 years old, Dory wrestled all of them and looked good doing it? On his website, he put up matches featuring him against Chris Harris, Rob Van Dam, and others.

Where do people like Harley Race and Dory Funk Jr. come from? They're like real life John Waynes. To have the kind of longevity in their business, you need to do something right. It's never been a problem for them.

There's also something else about Harley, Dory, Bruno, Ivan Koloff, Nick Bockwinkel, and the other legends that I've had the chance to interview. Everyone knows who they are: every performer I've interviewed is familiar with them as the greats from the past.

I'd say that's a pretty good indication that there's a lot to learn from wrestling history. Think about it. Everything is built on something else. Every star you see today was inspired by a great performer from yesterday. As newcomers join the industry, the best way for them to reach another level is to take something that worked before them and bring it to a new level. The only way to progress in wrestling, it seems, is to know who came before you.

That's where, for some, the stigma of a bitter veteran comes from. People assume that those who complain about today's wrestling have an axe to grind. In reality, many wrestlers just want to see the sport they love be the best it can be. It's about telling a story. When done in the proper context, moves need to make sense. The most common complaint you'll hear from both today's top stars and yesterday's legends is that too many guys go out in the ring and try to get all their moves in before the match is over, that what they do takes place out of context.

It's like going to see an action movie that features nonstop explosions. Yeah, things blow up, but there's no point.

Good storytelling isn't old school or new school. It just is. You can tell a good story with no moonsaults or five — if you know when to do them. That's where proper training comes in.

Training shouldn't be a problem, right? Wrong again. The desire to break into the business they love leads many wrestlers to make ill-advised decisions. In some cases, people just don't do research.

Don't believe me? Get this.

We have a MySpace page set up for ClubWWI and we actually get messages from young wrestlers asking if they can "work one of WWI's cards." No kidding. Someone actually wrote this: "Hey. Hit me up if you need midgets."

It took — no joke — an hour for me to figure out that the guy thought we were a wrestling promotion. My mind went in a million directions at once.

So, yeah, there're plenty of young guys out there who don't really get the need to properly check the background of those they get involved with. And that's just where the problems begin.

Now I'm not saying that you had to have been a WWE Champion to be a great trainer. Rip Rogers is one of the most respected out there, especially among those he's trained. He wasn't a main-eventer, and that's not the point. It's this: if your new trainer lies to you, it might be time to stop payment on that check, right? Les Thatcher, the owner of one-time WWE developmental territory Heartland Championship Wrestling, told me a story that would make anyone question Darwinism: "I had a guy tell me one time, 'Well, my trainer was one of the original Assassins.' I said, 'Really? Was it Tom or Jody?' Tom Ernesto or Joe Hamilton? He says, 'No . . . it was Herb Schmidt.' I said, 'I hate to give you bad news, but not only was he not one of the original, but he wasn't one of the top 500 Assassins.'"

I'd be shocked, except for the fact that, as I mentioned, I was offered midgets on MySpace . . .

It doesn't take much to find out where the reputable schools are or who the reputable teachers are. Wrestling's young stars, if they took the time to learn about a man like Les Thatcher, wouldn't get into Herb Schmidt situations. Les, much like the other trainers I mentioned, is one of the friendliest people you'll ever speak to. A young student merely has to walk up to him and ask a question to get an in-depth answer from a man who has worked with the best in the industry. Instead, many young guys and girls find themselves chasing their tails for years because they don't know how to do a Google search.

When you consider how few places there are to work in the United States, you quickly realize how important it is to get good training. Find someone reputable: if something he says is untrue, don't tell yourself he's "working" you . . .

He's not. He's just lying.

CHAPTER THREE

THE GOOD OL' BOYS

"It's not a gimmick and it's not an angle. There are legitimately crazy guys in wrestling . . . guys like Ricky Morton. But if you take guys like that out of the business, well then, to me, you don't have a business. . . . It's hard to portray the image of an outlaw unless you are one. That's what this business is built on. It's kind of like the carnival. You get guys, you know, that have been in prison for 20 years for hijacking an airplane or, you know, just outlandish stuff. People you run across in this business . . . bounty hunters. You just get it from all walks of life. That's the trade-off. The promoters want a more regular guy, who goes home to his wife and kids. That's great. You also need the guys that stay out until nine or ten in the morning. Now I know that probably ain't politically correct to say right now, you know. The spotlight's on us now, but you don't think there's a football player out there, somewhere, doing worse things than wrestlers?"
— **Bull Buchanan**

Nothing will make you feel more connected with wrestling's grass-roots than interviewing one of its ornery Southerners. Many performers from the U.S. South are known for being the type of guy who'll knock you out if you step to them. They'll fight you and your friends and family and anyone else you want to load in the pickup. Like Tracy Smothers told me, "I might not win, but I'll give 'em a fight."

Before I say anything else, let me tell you about the most important thing I've learned about wrestlers from the South: they enunciate on television. This is no knock on their accent, because,

God knows, to people not from New York, I probably have one too. But man, in the case of Ricky Morton, I didn't even realize it was him when he picked up the phone. He sounded like Boomhauer from *King of the Hill*, and I never saw it coming.

Ricky Morton

Fans the world over know Ricky Morton as the grinning Rock 'n' Roll Expresser who dropkicked his way into the hearts of young girls through 1980s. But a guy like Ricky didn't survive in those southern territories by letting people walk all over him. The best example of this was when I asked him about a dispute he had with UWF promoter Hermie Sadler. He explained why he was still going to use the plane ticket to Hermie's event without appearing on his card.

"I did pick the phone up to say, 'Did you get me a hotel room? I'll be there.' . . . Because I was going there to slap the living fuck out of him in front of all them boys. Tell ya the truth. I was gonna bitchslap the dogfuck out of him to let him understand he ain't gonna talk to me that way. But then after a couple of days, after I cooled down, I just called him that morning and said, 'Kiss my ass. I'm not coming . . .' You got to know what you're doing to run a wrestling business. What does Hermie Sadler know? His shows were all the shits. Everybody told me it was fuckin' horrible. And before you can be a promoter, at least you have to qualify to be in a goddamn race if you're a racecar driver. He didn't qualify. And then when he did qualify, I bet he didn't finish the motherfucker and never fuckin' won! So y'all can take that any way you want to. . . . He has no fuckin' business being a promoter in this business, because he has no clue. And Hermie, if you're listening to this, I'm not trying to be mean. I'm just trying to tell you the fuckin' truth."

After trying to decipher this, I called Dr. Tom Prichard. Tom, who is from Tennessee, knew Morton. I figured he could help me figure out a few things. His response? It was the same he says whenever I tell him who I've just interviewed: "Ah . . . How was Ricky?"

Tom's always responds that way when I tell him about my latest guest. I could tell Tom that I interviewed Elvis Presley and he wouldn't bat an eyelash. He'd say, "Ah . . . How was E?"

I told him Morton was great, but said, "There's something I don't get about you Southerners."

Tom replied, "Us Southerners?"

I said, "Yeah. He threatened to 'slap the dogfuck' out of Hermie Sadler."

"Okay."

See? His eyelashes never moved.

"Yeah . . . so what exactly is 'dogfuck'?"

Tom answered me so matter-of-factly that it made me feel silly.

"Dogfuck is what you slap out of somebody."

I see.

Tracy Smothers and Chris Candido in action

Ricky isn't alone. Tracy Smothers is another guest people ask me about. I've never been able to figure out Smothers. Some call him crazy; some call him half-crazy. Either way, he's one of the most enigmatic guys you'll meet in wrestling.

The thing about Tracy Smothers is that the first time I saw him, much like Ricky Morton, he was a grinning good guy with a tag partner. As a member of WCW's Wide Eyed Southern Boys and Young Pistols, Smothers was the happy-go-lucky babyface.

When I spoke with him, he was an angry, scrapping veteran who challenged the following people to a fight during his interview:

Vince McMahon,

John Bradshaw Layfield,

Kurt Angle,

Stephanie McMahon (she should be bitchslapped . . . like she did to Jim Ross),

Daniel Puder,

Wrestling Observer's Dave Meltzer,

"The Supposed English Wrestler" who posts on his message boards, and

"All the Faggots Who Hide Behind Fake Names" on message boards.

While he expressed his anger for WWE's biggest names and bizarrely claimed "Dave Meltzer could whoop JBL and Kurt Angle at the same time," Tracy's most vicious ire was directed at his own message board . . .

> "Guys get on my message board talkin' shit. They don't know anything about me. They have these goofy names they come up with. Come see me. I really feel that way too, because I'm from the old school. And I learned the hard way. But I learned one thing, you have respect for this business or you're not worth a fuck."

What else can you say? It's all spelled out, right there. Smothers doesn't play games and, while even he admits that many of the things he's said are done for publicity, he'll still knock you silly if you get in his face.

There's something genuine about people like Smothers. The fact that he openly admits to wanting to publicize himself shows that. I mean, how often does a guy say, "I'll fight anyone! I'm not trying for publicity . . . well, maybe a bit?" The whole story with guys like Smothers is out in the open. There's no politics or gossip. He'll just walk up to you and swing.

The other thing about guys like Tracy, Ricky Morton, and countless other veterans is that they got to work more often, and in front of more people, than we can imagine. In a territory system that left many dates open for wrestlers to book themselves, guys like these worked constantly, and they still do that today. Even without a WWE contract, it's nothing for these rasslers to work almost every day. It's just the way they live.

That's unfortunate for many young wannabe stars looking to make their name, and it's something that's come up a lot. After all, with so many people complaining that today's wrestlers don't know psychology, or how to call a spot, we tend to forget that they have fewer opportunities to practice in front of a live crowd. Today, with so much competition from established veterans, it's simply harder to find regular independent work. Today's young wrestlers are at the mercy of the few promotions still operating.

It was one of the true hot buttons for Tracy Smothers. He was unhappy about the lack of dates available to wrestlers, and he put the blame squarely on Vince McMahon. Why? Well because, silly, it's his fault. . . .

When Vinnie Mac's WWE expanded, it became a giant, corporate Pac Man, eating up all the territorial ghosts in his path. With them went the jobs and dates that guys like Smothers rely on. But while McMahon is to blame, you can't stay too angry. Had it not been Vince, it would have been someone else. After all, it's the twenty-first century. We live in the age of the internet and 50,000 TV channels. If you believe the territories would have survived if only Vince had stayed away, you probably also believe 8-track tapes would have survived if only Sony hadn't introduced the Walkman.

It still stinks for the guys, though. Bull Buchanan explained it in a way that really made me think about what it was like before McMahonivision: "I heard Dick Murdoch say one time that he flew over his house I think five or six times before he ever got to go home. Those guys were on the road 30 days at a time; they'd come home, and go back out for another 30 days."

Can you imagine? There's a reason why guys like that are respected. The life of a wrestler is tough, no matter what generation you come from, but there was something extra rough about the days before cable.

Bull is another southern-born scrapper and, if it isn't obvious from his quotes, he's a strong believer in the smash-mouth style of

Bull Buchanan

wrestling. Even masked behind his different WWE gimmicks, fans of his work in Right to Censor, the Truth Commission, or the B2 gimmick (booyah!) saw that. Whether in a tie or an army outfit, don't mess with Barry Buchanan, or he'll kick your face in.

When I heard that Bull was a fan of my site, I was surprised. D-Lo Brown, a ClubWWI audio host, mentioned that Buchanan would set up his laptop in Japan and read stuff that we had on the site to all the boys in the room. Apparently, we were a big hit in All Japan and, in Barry's words, the boys would fall on the floor laughing. Given that we did so much parody, I took this as a compliment.

Much like D-Lo's "Lo-Down," or Orlando Jordan's "Club OJ," Bull Buchanan took the reigns of his own audio report. "The Bullpen" debuted and Buchanan showed that he had an eye for the business that only comes from years of being a part of it.

He loves the business, and that comes through on the air. Many of his shows seemingly have no direction as they begin. I'll start off by saying, "So, how are things by you?" And from there, things evolve over the next hour: about trainers, WWE stories, what makes wrestling work, and more. He's one of the easiest people to talk to when it comes to the specifics of the wrestling business, and he ranks up there with Les Thatcher and Tom Prichard when it comes to wrestling theory.

And he doesn't try to schmooze anyone, either. That's his trademark. Maybe it's the fact that he's from the South (David Young calls him, "Andy Griffith on steroids"), but Bull doesn't . . . well, bullshit. His opinions are unfiltered, and the honesty he offers is something I respect tremendously.

I was especially concerned about that when we started adding new audio shows. Dr. Tom Prichard's show, "Tuesdays With Tom," had never been sugarcoated. While there was no WWE bashing for the sake of WWE bashing, Prichard still spoke out on what he thought was poorly done. Everything was on the table and he didn't kiss butt to get into McGoodGraces. Eventually . . . they hired him back. It was a good indication that you don't have to worry about what you say as long as it's fair.

Dr. Tom Prichard

Kevin Kelly, former co-host of *Raw*, said it best in the first edition of his segment. It's something that should be applied to any prospective guest.

"If you are worried about Vince calling and hiring you," he said, "don't bother doing this show. Don't waste Guttman's time. Don't waste the fans' time. Don't waste anybody's time."

I love that. No statement better sums up what I've been trying to do. Either show up real or don't show up at all. This ain't Hands Across America.

Which somehow brings me to my original point. Having straight shooters on air really helps. I'd rather have Ricky Morton curse for hours on end than have to figure out how to structure a press release out of an interview with Johnny Jobhunter.

If you think Ricky's a tough cookie, could you imagine the guys he trained? Me neither. That's why I needed to interview David "Kid" Kash. For those who aren't familiar, Kash has been a champion in ECW, WWE, and TNA. He's also had plenty to say.

In one of the most imaginative ways to get out of a contract ever, Kid decided that if TNA wouldn't release him, he'd force their hand. Despite being on the payroll, Kash did a series of interviews accusing TNA of everything from favoritism to . . . gay favors. According to Dave, it was the only way out. Once he was done dishing the dirt on his then-employers, he got the phone call.

"Jerry Jarrett called and asked, 'Do you still want that release?' I said, 'Yeah.' He said, 'You got it five minutes ago.' I said, 'Fax me the hard copy.'"

I really like Dave, for the same reason I like Ricky, Tracy, Tom, and Barry. There was no wondering where I stood with him. I knew at any point during the interview if I said something stupid, he'd tell me. When he didn't, I knew it wasn't because he was being polite; it was because I didn't say something stupid.

The thing that may have separated Kid from Morton and Smothers, though, was his delivery. I spoke to Bull about him a few days later and he called Kash a "walking comedy act." Buchanan was right. Unlike Ricky's excitability or Tracy's subdued aggression, Dave said things in a way that just made you laugh. For instance, when talking about TNA's lack of respect for performers, he said, "These assholes don't remember that if it wasn't for the wrestler, there wouldn't be any fans to come watch the show, you know?"

I know that doesn't read as funny, but it's the way he said it that cracked me up. He didn't say "assholes" like it was an insult — it was so matter-of-fact you'd think it was the name of some guy he was talking about. It's as if the people working in the TNA office were named Bob and Cindy Asshole. There's nothing like a straight-shooting, ornery southern boy to remind you what the wrestling business is truly built on.

But wait. There's a flipside to all this. . . .

I get to interview *Playboy* models. How insane is that? It's one of the most fascinating things about this business. Like Bull said, the variety of people you can meet in this industry is mind blowing. Week to week, I never know what conversation I'm going to have. And it can change on a dime. Don't believe me?

End of December 2007, I was speaking to Ron "The Truth" Killings about his rap music roots and what Easy E was really like. The very next, I was interviewing 84-year-old Mae Young about her plans to fight Triple H's daughter, Aurora Rose, on her one-hundredth birthday. Two weeks later? UFC Hall of Famer Dan Severn is telling me about how he trains policemen to fight. Next, I'm learning about the Iditarod from pro dogsledder Paul Ellering. In May of 2008, Ahmed Johnson told me about being in the Bloods street gang.

I mean, seriously. And the strangest part is that it's actually common. Because of all the different personalities who get involved in wrestling, I'm more likely to get someone who's unique each week, than to get someone who's similar to other guests.

When I'm asked about how things vary from one week to the next, I always point to episode 33. That week, we welcomed Nora "Molly Holly" Greenwald: the quintessential good girl, too sweet to cuss. Almost every wrestling fan you talk to will tell you there's a special place in his (or in some cases, her) heart for Nora. After all, she's sugar and spice and everything nice.

Episode 34? "Big Poppa Pump" Scott Steiner. He likes to talk about giving orgasms to his freaky ladies.

Like I said, the variety is probably my favorite part of doing these interviews. I get to speak with and learn from so many diverse people. I've never been able to approach two interviews the same way. In a business all about personality, you don't make a name for yourself by having a reputation or character that's too similar to someone else's.

I especially hope listeners hear that in the shoots. What I'm doing is not just about backstage dirt. Sure, that's part of the story. But what I'm really after are the characters behind the characters. When you really know the wrestler, know their motivation, it makes it easier to understand the hows and whys of what they've been involved in. You quickly learn why someone might take exception to the way Eric Bischoff spoke about them. You understand why Buff Bagwell gets heat. And you get what it means when someone says, "That's Ole being Ole."

Once you get to understand the wrestler, you begin to understand their stories. After all, it's easier to analyze gossip about people you know than people you don't, right?

All of this has given me the opportunity to learn about things I never would have otherwise. I've been schooled in everything from doing a *Playgirl* shoot by Big Vito, to what it was like filming a scene in *Live Free or Die Hard* by Damien Demento. And clearly, I can't imagine any other way I'd run into a dogsledder on Long Island.

Hearing the stars' takes on the most controversial wrestling stories allows fans the rare opportunity to make up their own minds. But of course, at no time do I claim that what is said by my guests is always 100% true. . . . That's not the point. But given how long each of my guests speaks for, it's pretty hard for them to keep up a façade. I like to think that, by the end of our discussion, almost every guest has been forced out from behind the wall of their personas and reluctance.

Of course, while everyone I speak to is unique, they all share a common bond. They're "in the business." It's something you and I, as fans, can't say. They've had the chance to work in the industry and, when that happens, they earn the right to express informed opinions.

It's inevitable. We all have opinions about our work, specifically and generally. There're guys working at McDonald's who have theories on the best way to salt fries, just like there're bank tellers who disagree with their boss's managerial style. Wrestlers are no different.

Beyond their personality, history, and reputation, when you begin to understand a performer's take on the wrestling industry, you can start to analyze behind-the-scenes situations from their perspective. There is no better way to expose the motivation behind someone's backstage maneuvers than to know what they believe is right for the industry.

Forget revenge and sabotage. The most common reason why performers get involved in backstage politics is because they truly believe they know what's best for business. It's the reason why people like Kevin Nash, Eric Bischoff, Jerry Lawler, Vince Russo, Kevin Sullivan, and tons of others have done what they've done during their long careers.

The bond that every wrestler shares? They have the same job. Chances are, they've worked with many of the same people. At the end of the day, they also share, hopefully, the same basic training. Together, they can talk about their opinions on crowd psychology, character development, match pacing, and tons of other topics most fans never think much about.

When you look at things in this way, it takes a lot of the mystery and vicarious kick out of backstage rumors. It also helps clarify some of them. I've gotten e-mails from readers who read news items on wrestling newssites saying they only finally "get it" because of something one of my guests has said on ClubWWI.

I'm not trying to cure cancer or influence the race to the White House. I'm writing about wrestling — something I've always loved. I'm grateful every day that I have the chance to do what I do. While I can point to all the different things about the business I love, I really can't pinpoint one thing specifically. I felt bad about this until I interviewed Al Snow: he showed me I'm not alone in not knowing.

> "People come up all the time, 'Oh. I've always wanted to be a wrestler.' I go, 'Why?' . . . If you can actually come up with a reason why you want to do this, then you probably shouldn't. The reason I say that — it sounds crazy, and I'm sure a lot of people are saying, 'What the hell's he talkin' about?' But if you were to ask me 26 years ago why I wanted to do it, I'd tell you, then, I don't know. I just know I wanted to do it. If you ask me now 26 years later, I still don't know. I just love doing it. I love doing it more than anything else. I've done all kinds of stuff. I've acted in movies. I've had a lot of different opportunities in many different avenues and venues in life. Nothing, absolutely nothing compares to getting the chance to do this. It's better than drugs. It's better than sex. It's better than anything. . . . It's the greatest high and it doesn't matter if there are five people in the audience, doesn't matter if there's five million. When you have those nights, it's just fantastic and it just keeps you going. . . . When you can explain it, maybe this isn't for you. Let's face it. Look at what you're doing for a living. Joey Matthews sent me a text and sometimes his wisdom is far beyond his years. He sent me a text that went, 'I fake-fight grown-ass men in underwear for money. I'm very good at it, but it seems immaterial and unimportant when you say it like that.' And I can't agree with him any more than that. If you can justify why you're fake-fighting grown-ass men for money, then you're probably making up a reason, or you really don't want to do this for the right reasons."

This statement, alone, probably best illustrates the ways wrestlers and fans are similar. In fact, they're really one and the same. Snow's words can be turned around and applied to why many fans love wrestling. After all, we *watch* grown-ass men in underwear fake-fight for money.

Sometimes it's a tough thing to wrap your head around, right? It sort of takes the bloom off the rose. . . . But we also almost always share Al's inability to explain the allure of wrestling. For many of us, when a friend asks what we like about the sport, there's an uncomfortable pause.

As I wrote in *World Wrestling Insanity*, for those who love it, no explanation is necessary. For those who don't, none will do.

In nearly every case, wrestlers are simply fans who wanted to partici- pate. Interview almost any established star and you'll hear stories about Dick the Bruiser, Lou Thesz, Bruno Sammartino, and the others who came before them. Why? Because they watched them on television in exactly the same way today's fans watch John Cena and Randy Orton. They were just like us.

Al Snow

And often they still are.

Don't get me wrong. Not every performer was a fanatic before breaking into the business. But even the ones that weren't, almost always become that way once they're in. It's impossible to work in the industry and not develop an appreciation for its past. The few who don't care don't seem to stick around long.

So yes, it might sound odd for a man who interviews wrestlers to say that it took interviewing wrestlers to teach him that fans and performers both simply love wrestling. But the fact is, that's true.

We just can't tell you why.

CHAPTER FOUR

THE OFFICE

Pssst. Hey, wanna know a secret? During the Monday Night Wars, I cheered for Eric Bischoff.

Yeah, I know we're not supposed to talk about it. After all, WCW lost. Now we learn about it like a history lesson, but back then, it was happening in real time. There were two sides, and WCW still had fans in the end. Hell, they had tons of fans throughout the whole thing. When Eric Bischoff went on *Nitro* and gave away *Raw* results, fans on the other side, WWF fans, freaked out.

And WCW fans laughed.

At least I did. Say whatever you want about the ethics of it, but it was the way things got done. Easy E wasn't the first one to use dirty tricks. He was just the first one to do it with style. When Vince McMahon pillaged the wrestling scene in the 1980s, he did it from behind his office door. Fans knew him as "the yellow-suit guy." Eric Bischoff manipulated the world of wrestling with a smile — on TV — with Hulk Hogan behind him.

It truly excited fans of all stripes. WWF had become quite stale by the mid-'90s. I mean, really, really stale. Okay, it was horrible. King Mabel. The Goon. Sean Waltman in a diaper. . . . Come on, I was tired of it and you were tired of it, and worse, I felt like I was falling out of love with it. It wasn't fun anymore. As I was growing up, it seemed like the World Wrestling Federation was growing . . . down.

World Championship Wrestling was no better. It was WWF lite. Sure, the matches were more entertaining, but the shows were equally lame. Hulk Hogan was trying another Hulkamania run and the company had a big helicopter landing strip on its ring mat. If there was anything staler than *Raw*, it was at the Center Stage Theater in Atlanta, where *WCW Saturday Night* was taped.

But then, miraculously, things changed. Scott Hall and Kevin Nash showed up and terrorized WCW as "outsiders" from "up north." And, miracle of miracles, Hogan became a bad guy, with a spray painted-on black beard, and telling everyone to "stick it." Almost overnight, the business had changed. Everywhere you looked, there were nWo shirts. Way before Austin 3:16 or ECW logos, there was the New World Order.

4 Life.

Too sweet.

Eric Bischoff and Hulk Hogan

When Eric Bischoff declared a holy war on all things WWF, it took professional wrestling to a level that no one thought possible. Fans got to watch a real feud play out, between entities that were something other than wrestlers. We watched multinational companies go at each other on a weekly basis.

Before this, apart from a few pathetic "We'll put on Clash of Champions the same day as *WrestleMania*" attempts, World Championship Wrestling had never really made a dent in the façade of the house that Vince built.

What Bischoff had masterminded worked, big time.

Everyone was hooked. After so many years, WCW finally had real direction; it was really targeting the World Wrestling Federation, and it was amazing. The tricks were dirty and the stakes were high. WCW *Nitro* gave away the results to WWF *Raw*'s taped shows; they mocked their roster; Eric even challenged Vince McMahon to a fight on a WCW pay-per-view. Sure, he and everyone else on the planet knew it wasn't going to happen — but it didn't matter, it was still crazy. To this day, Uncle Eric's speech calling out Vince McMahon remains one of wrestling's best. I quoted it in *World Wrestling Insanity*, and I'll quote it again here, because it truly signaled the birth of a new era in wrestling.

> There's no need for spins or dirt-sheets. We can settle this like true men, Vince. Just you, and me. You can do it . . . Come on, Vince. Step into the ring. Do what so many other people would love to do. Get your hands around my skinny little neck. You can do it . . . if you've got the guts. Do you, Vince? Have you got the guts to really show up? I do . . . Do you? Just think of it. Just think how great you'll feel if you're able to step into the ring and break my jaw . . . knock me out . . . snap an arm or a leg! Whatever you'd like, Vince! It's no big thing. But it takes guts. That's what it's gonna take, Vince. Have you got the guts, Vince? We'll find out . . . we'll be waiting for you, Vinnie Mac. With open arms.

Thing is, with this, it wasn't just WCW fans who were laughing. WWF fans were too. Ultimately, we were all along for the ride. It was like watching a poker game where the final two guys at the table are both all in. In the end, you don't care who wins or loses. You're not betting . . .

Sure, WCW lost. But the battle itself created the changes to the industry that still shape wrestling to this day. And the man most associated with the pop culture juggernaut that was WCW is Eric Bischoff. He's the poster child. Not Ric Flair. Not Sting. Not Lex Luger. Not P.N. News. Eric Bischoff. He could work for WWE until he's 300, but he'll forever be known as Mr. WCW.

I was proud of the interview I did with Eric in May 2007. It uncovered a real complexity to the man and, ultimately, humanized him. He had an enthusiasm about what he had done that gets lost in translation when people are trying to bury him for World Championship Wrestling's demise. Bischoff may have had his faults, but he truly loved what he was doing. Much like Kevin Nash, you could hear it in his voice. WCW was Bischoff's baby.

The other thing you'll realize if you listen to that interview is that he's unflinchingly honest. He says what he thought and felt was best for business — and clearly, back then, if it was best for business he'd tell you twice. He took no prisoners. That's just how he was.

Sometimes that can come off kind of . . . well, crappy. There's a real self-assurance about Eric Bischoff, and it can be somewhat abrasive. Even interviewing him, I could pick up on it. Working for him, I'm sure it would have been magnified ten-fold. He's the type of guy you'd like to hang out with at a bar; he's also the kind of guy who might make you want to hang yourself if you had to work for him.

Ultimately, Eric has done well. Losing the Monday Night Wars could have been a fatal blow to someone in his position. Bischoff didn't miss a beat. He's continued to be a success in his wrestling career, marketing work, and production ventures. Hell, without him, we wouldn't have known that Scott Baio was 46 and pregnant . . .

When I first came across a number for Eric Bischoff, I was unsure if it would even still be good. Over time, I'd become well acquainted with the lady who tells me that a number's been disconnected. (Her name's Mary. She has a different accent in different states. She usually hangs up after only one sentence.) So when I called Eric, I was prepared to get Mary . . . I certainly wasn't expecting him to pick up.

"Hello?"

Uh . . . wow. I knew it was Bischoff with just the one word. In my head I heard, "We'll be waiting for you, Vinnie Mac."

"Eric? This is James Guttman from WorldWrestlingInsanity.com. How are you doing?"

"I'll be better when you tell me how you got this number."

Okay, not fun. That's all I need. The nWo and Jason Hervey would be sent to my house to kill me. I figured the whole interview wasn't going to happen anyway, so I told him how I had run into someone he had worked with outside of wrestling who said I should reach out to him about my site. I then patiently waited for him to slam down the phone.

"That's a good answer. Okay. So, what's up?"

From that moment on, Eric Bischoff was, well, awesome.

What I really admired about Eric was the fact that he had high hopes for everything he did. His goal was always to take things all the way. Especially in wrestling. He stormed into WCW and ran over those who stood in his way. The self-inspired song "Stand Back" that Vince McMahon sang in the 1980s could have applied to Bischoff too. There was no coddling or diplomacy to him: Bischoff don't play that.

When talking about his dealings with the company's old guard, he made it clear that the days that they were still trying to hang on to were long gone. He talked about how Bill Watts and the era of Mid-South were over. The wrestling business had to change. Seemed like a fair assessment, right? Time moves on. Nothing for old-schoolers to be upset about . . .

Oh, but then he also called Watts a "buckethead" and "one of the biggest jokes that ever happened in this business, at least in the latter part of his career." So that's . . . I, uh . . . I can see how that might sting a little.

The whole situation created what Eric called a "shitstorm." His explanation of why this storm began cracked me up: "If you have a kid and your kid's ugly, you know your kid's ugly. But you don't want to have somebody else tell you your kid's ugly."

So Eric marched right in and started pointing at WCW's buckteeth and deformed ears. Nice kid you got there, Buckethead.

Here's the really crazy thing about the interview. Less than a month earlier, I had Ole Anderson on. As you you'll read later, that discussion was . . . less than wonderful. Since Ole was one of the people Eric was talking about, I couldn't help but agree with his analogy.

In my opinion — and this is strictly my opinion — normally, it's best to try to suck it up and work with others for a greater good. In this case, though, I don't think that would have worked for Bischoff. Guys like Bill Watts and Ole Anderson didn't get where they were by schmoozing with some Minnesota coffee boy. They did what they did, end of story.

In some cases, you need a slap in the face, a fresh perspective, to help you create something new and special. Bischoff was that slap in the face, and he was able to guide the floundering WCW in a new direction — even if there were some unfortunate casualties along the way.

Case in point? Ric Flair. The Nature Boy is . . . wow. Flair's a crazy subject. I could devote a whole chapter to Ric, without even ever having him on as a guest. His name comes up much more than you'd ever expect.

And many times what's said is not so good . . .

Bruno Sammartino

"No, I don't respect Ric Flair. I don't respect him at all. Here's a guy we all heard about — which I couldn't believe — he exposes himself on an airplane! He got sued for it. Remember that? He used to get a kick out of jumping on a bar at saloons and mooning everybody in the joint. Here's a guy who almost got arrested and went to jail 25 years ago for not paying income taxes, and Crocket Sr. worked out a deal with the IRS to take so much out of his pay. . . . Then I found out a year ago, the same thing happened all over again. What, is this a guy to be looked up to? Give me a break! Sounds to me like he's a real misfit."

— Bruno Sammartino

"There's nobody who inspired me more to work my ass off to make it than Ric Flair. Because Ric Flair did everything he could to try to hold me down."

— Diamond Dallas Page

"He's a pussy, man. If people could see these guys behind the curtain, they'd be amazed."

— Scott Steiner

It might not be popular with some fans, but I could go on like this for a while. For some reason, Flair has many detractors within the industry. Issues people might have with him behind the scenes, however, don't take away from the respect he commands for his work in the ring. While some might not care for him personally, his name comes up as much as anyone's when I ask guests who they wish they could have worked with.

Personally, I could listen to 1000 people tell me that Ric Flair is the devil incarnate — and I'd still jump at the chance to interview him. He is, after all, the Nature Boy.

Eric's feud with Slick Ric is the stuff of legend. And it went beyond the personal. Famous for his rant about wanting Flair's family to starve, Bischoff has at times been labeled the boss that wanted to destroy the Nature Boy. Eric was supposed to be like Jim Herd, only you replace the jokes about his background in Pizza Hut management with jokes about fetching coffee for Verne Gagne.

So when Bischoff spoke about Naitch, I was truly surprised there was no venom. It sounded like he ultimately *did* respect Flair, just not as much as Flair might have liked.

Easy E made it clear: "There were times, quite frankly, when I thoroughly enjoyed being with Ric; and some of the best experiences I've had on a personal level in this business, I've had with Ric Flair. And there were other times where if I was on top of a tall building with Ric Flair and I could somehow throw him over the edge, I would have."

In the end, Uncle Eric's management style and occasional smugness work in many cases, but don't in others. In terms of his wrestling management career, I definitely think that he was a victim of circumstances beyond his control as his WCW dreams died. He had all his ducks in a row and could have continued to make an impact: if only a TV deal had gone through, there might still be a Monday *Nitro* today.

I firmly believe that had things just gone in a slightly different direction, I might be writing about my ClubWWI interview with Vince McMahon and the online community would be bitching about *Nitro*'s lack of competition.

Bischoff and McMahon call to mind the other side of the spectrum, someone like Tod Gordon. The creator of ECW back in the early 1990s, Tod was a part of making some of my favorite wrestling moments. The first time I ever saw the renegade promotion's true grit was during the post-main event press conference for *The Night the Line Was Crossed*. In a mocking gesture, Terry Funk handed his ECW Championship to a complaining Shane Douglas to try to shut the younger man up. Douglas, disgusted, called him an "old piece of shit" and threw it back. They started brawling, people held them back, and Tod Gordon was front and center with a microphone. The whole thing seemed real.

Now that's some crazy-ass pro wrestling. No one was doing that at the time. Like I said earlier, remember — King Mabel, The Goon, Sean Waltman in a diaper . . .

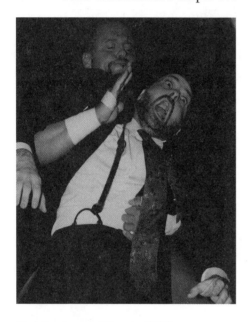

Tod Gordon and Tazz in ECW

When Gordon eventually got out of ECW, Paul Heyman officially became the company's universally lionized brainchild. And Heyman did a tremendous job, bringing Extreme to unimaginable heights. However, even Paul would agree that Tod was a tremendous part of ECW's history, creation, and execution, especially during its most important, formative years. Unfortunately, because WWE owns everything "ECW" now, they get to write, or rewrite its history. And that's why the whole Tod Gordon saga becomes kind of confusing, I guess, because he's barely mentioned. It's a shame, too; people may drink "Paul Heyman's Kool-Aid," but Tod Gordon bought Paul-E the mixing bowl and helped to create the recipe. . . .

When I caught up with him, Gordon was running Pro Wrestling Unplugged. PWU runs out of the old ECW arena in Philly and features both established stars and up-and-comers. In many ways, it feels more like the original ECW than WWE's version.

Here's the thing about Tod Gordon: he's got a real passion for what he does. In fact, he has so much passion that it's hard to explain. Talking to him about something he promoted conjures up stories that sound more like an excited fan telling you what he saw at the matches, than what you'd expect from the man who actually put it all together.

Gordon is, in my opinion, the quintessential wrestling fan. He loves it; he loves the workers; he loves the atmosphere; he loves the fans. Tod Gordon can take five dollars and put together a show that will rival anything anyone can book. It's what makes him great at what he does. He truly feels it, truly loves it.

The difference between Tod and someone like Eric Bischoff is like night and day. Eric is the high society, slick, wheeler-dealer; Gordon is grassroots, a man of the people. The irony, though, is that at the end of the day, they're both considered "office."

> "The office call it 'the business,' but they get real mad when the boys call it a business. It's like, hey, it's not just a 'business' for you. It's business for everybody."
> — **Kevin Nash**

But in Tod Gordon's case, that's not true. He treats young stars almost like students, and his top stars, like Too Cold Scorpio, are friends. If wrestling had a true mom and pop promoter, it was Tod Gordon.

This just shows how diverse the wrestling industry is. It's impossible to paint everyone with the same brush: you shouldn't do it with wrestlers, and you clearly shouldn't do it with promoters. I mean, if you're going to put Bischoff, McMahon, and Gordon in the same "office" category and marvel at *their* differences, then wait until I throw another past guest into the mix. . . .

Yup, the great, the notorious Vicious Vincent appeared on "JG's Radio Free Insanity." It happened in October of 2005 and it was a shoot interview 12 years in the making. Who's Vicious Vincent, you ask? Well, let me tell you . . .

When I was in tenth grade, I came across an ad in *New York*

Newsday for a local radio show. Entitled "Vicious Vincent's World of Wrestling," the geared-to-kids broadcast featured guests from both WWE and WCW. Needless to say, this was like Christmas for a young wrestling fan in the days before the internet. Just a few days later, I sat down in front of a giant stereo system that would seem archaic today, and tuned into my first episode.

Hosted by "Vicious" Vincent, a bearded New Yawka with an Undertaker-like hat, the World of Wrestling was a weekly chance to hear banter on the industry. Alongside high-pitched co-host "The Mat Rat" and Skull "Ten Years Before I Become Vito in WWE" Von Kruss, the way Vicious Vince covered wrestling was unlike any one else.

As any wrestling fan knows, when it comes to the world of rasslin', we don't do things in half measures, we go all out. We don't just play wrestling video games, we spend hours recreating wrestlers and matches. It's the kind of all-in mentality you find in any subculture, I guess. Cult-like followings foster all kinds of insanity: how else can you explain grown men and women running around with Klingon weapons or dressed as Ewoks?

So, I didn't just listen to Vicious Vince — I called in every chance I got.

"Let's get back to the lines, Mat Rat. James from Lindenhurst. Go ahead . . ."

This was my first experience with wrestling interview shows. And Vicious Vincent — you all know him as Vince Russo — featured many different guests. In fact, years before he would get all nice and shiny and appear on *Nancy Grace*, Marc "Johnny B. Badd" Mero graced Vince's airwaves. It was right after the epic Clash of the Champions where Scotty "Raven" Flamingo knocked him out in a boxing match, all thanks to a glove full of water. The show, keeping up kayfabe, featured Johnny's thoughts on the subject. He stayed in character and treated it as real. Even the listeners played along.

I called in.

"Hi Johnny? How can you say you're going to kick Scotty Flamingo's booty with your Tutti Frutti when, from what I saw, he kicked your butt with his uppercut?"

Bam. Oh, snap. You see what I did there? You see what I did? He got served!

But seriously, though, Vince's show was an inspiration to me. He was always polite and accommodating. There were many times I called his video store to ask him questions about wrestling. He always answered and never blew me off. I remember how much that meant to me, and that's why, today, I try to respond to just about every e-mail I get. That's just one thing I got from Vince Russo.

Before long, I was taking bus trips with the Vicious Vincent army. We went all over for local house shows and I even won a free ticket to see Halloween Havoc 1992 with the whole group. About 20 of us headed down and sat three rows in. At the time, I never imagined that saying, "I sat in the third row of Halloween Havoc 1992 with Vince Russo" would ever be a big deal. But it is.

Vince and his radio crew also hosted live, on-location shows. I'll never forget the one set up at the Whitey Ford Baseball Clinic. It was one of those fun-time places with batting cages and skeet ball. Vince, Matrat, and Big Vito showed up and did their show live, while we sat and watched.

After the event, everyone hung out and the guys interacted with the listeners. Skull, sitting at a table, was arm-wrestling a young fan. In an effort to be nice, he faked strain and then let him win.

Being a jerk, I said, "And that's why Skull's a jobber."

The glare I got scared the piss out of me. I decided right then and there to stay off the bad side of Vito Lograsso.

My resolution lasted all of about ten minutes. Shortly after, during a basketball game between The Show and The Listeners, I accidentally knocked him in the mouth trying to block a pass. Skull stopped, wiped his mouth, and stared at me like I was insane. I really expected him to kill me at that point. If I were him, *I* probably would have killed me.

Vito was cool, though. In fact, years later, when I finally had the chance to interview him, he remembered his Vicious Vincent days fondly. He, like his former broadcast partner, had definitely come full circle and made good. After struggling through some hard times, Lograsso got noticed in ECW, WCW, and WWE. Things ended up working out well for him, and he seemed to be happy with his career.

But a good comeback story always needs some kind of low point. Shortly after Whitey Ford's, Russo's luck started to go bad and soon his show was on its way out. Rumors swirled and things looked bad for "Vish" — it only got worse when he wound up closing his store, Long Island's Will The Thrill Video. I was there the day it closed and bought two VHS tapes for a buck each. I figured that would be the last time I ever saw Vince Russo.

Five years later . . . he revolutionized the wrestling industry.

Say whatever you want about Vicious Vincent, but you can't deny this: the period in which he was working for WWF was pure gold. I rushed home to watch *Raw* every week, and if I couldn't be there, I taped it. It brought must-see TV to a new level. I never missed the World Wrestling Federation when Vinnie Ru and Ed Ferrara were writing.

Today, I sometimes forget when the shows are on.

When I finally reconnected with Russo in December of 2005, I dropped him an e-mail and told him who I was. "Not sure if you remember me. James from Lindenhurst . . ." I then told him about the site and asked him if he'd be up for an interview. His reply was great: "Hey James. Of course I remember! VICIOUS VINCENT NEVER FORGETS!"

Now before you roll your eyes and say, "Oh great, you interviewed this guy who inspired you . . . I'm sure he could do no wrong, right?" Wrong. Russo didn't get a free ride. I asked him about all his high points . . . and the low ones.

Vince wasn't the goose that laid the golden eggs each time out. Some of the stuff Vince was a part of in WCW was putrid. Everyone always comes down on him for this, his failings in World Championship Wrestling. They claim that it's because Vince McMahon had final say over his WWF material — that's what made it work so well.

Now this is a charge that didn't sit well with Vicious Vincent: "That's why there's the stigma — 'Oh, Vince McMahon edited everything Vince Russo did. It was Vince McMahon.' You know

Vince Russo in WCW

what, bro? That is so old. . . . And if Vince is the genius, then where are his seven ratings today?"

I've always believed that Russo's point is valid. While many see his jump to WCW as part of what lead to their decline, it didn't exactly send WWE hurtling toward better things. In the end, in my opinion, Vince just worked better in the WWF environment. Sometimes people perform better when they're enjoying their surroundings.

This doesn't mean that Vince McMahon was the driving force behind Russo's best work. But perhaps it indicates that things were too loose for Russo in WCW. Who knows, maybe too much creative power caused him to bite off more than he could chew. Or maybe there were just too many people to please — on both sides of the camera — and too many extenuating circumstances.

While I don't subscribe to the theory that McMahon was the reason Russo's material was top notch, I also won't subscribe to the theory that Russo's WCW material was simply "misunderstood." Some of it was just painful to watch. However, when you factor in that, as I mentioned to Kevin Nash, "the shows were bad" during a number of different points in WCW history, you have to wonder whether there's a pattern.

In discussing this with many who worked for World Championship Wrestling, I've discovered the setup there wasn't really conducive to creativity. Between standards and practices and Turner, there were just too many people to please before the shows even aired. The company was already a mess on many different levels when Vince Russo landed there. Moving, as far as I can see, might have been Russo's biggest mistake of all.

At the time, though, his reasoning was sound. Russo explained to me that near the end of his WWF days, he picked a copy of *Cigar*

Aficionado that featured an interview with his boss. Vince McMahon put the credit for the company's success on the shoulders of his son, Shane. Vinnie Ru read this as he was just taking a break from a nine-hour day of writing WWF television. . . .

So, yeah, I can imagine the motivation behind, "Screw you guys, I'm going home."

Hindsight being 20/20, leaving was a mistake. And though a part of me can clearly understand Russo's reasoning, another part wonders why he was so surprised to see all the credit go to someone named McMahon. After all, WWE doesn't roll credits at the end of the shows. If you asked the casual fan who writes wrestling for TV, most would probably say Vince McMahon. I always thought that was a given. The structure of the company's public persona isn't very conducive to sharing credit.

That's not to say that Vince Russo's story had a bad ending. Vince found religion, changed his life, and got a job he's happy with at TNA. The hometown boy has definitely made good.

Back in 1992, I never would have guessed that one day Vicious Vincent would truly be able to say that it was *his* world of wrestling. He just had to get back up after being knocked down. And no matter what you think of his creativity, you have to admit it says a lot about his character.

I'm not sure I could dust myself off and carry on as many times as he — and other people involved in wrestling — has had to.

CHAPTER FIVE

BLOOPERS, BLEEPS, AND OLE ANDERSON

Many people have asked why I created ClubWWI.com. For the first 36 episodes of "Radio Free Insanity," it didn't exist. Before ClubWWI, each week a new interview would go up and the old one would come down and disappear into the ether, never to be heard from again.

The Club opened in September 2006. And the short answer why is: to make money.

Most people just leave it at that. They figure I'm greedy, and that I like to sit in my giant house made of diamond dust and throw hundred dollar bills in the air while cackling about the billions I make from interviewing wrestlers. . . .

And if you believe that, there's not much more I can say.

For those who have their feet planted on the ground of this planet, there's actually more to it. Okay, sure, providing free audio costs money on my end. Every time someone downloads a show from WorldWrestlingInsanity.com, our web host clocks it. Once we reach the maximum for the month, we're done. No more audio. No more pictures. No more site. Done.

Unless, of course, yours truly forks over more cash.

At first, naturally, I struggled to keep my interviews relatively short. By January 2006, I was timing them and trying to keep each one under 30 minutes. I never wanted to split a guest's interview into two shows. I've seen five- or six- or one-hundred-part interviews, and it never made any sense to me. I wanted people to hear a wrestler's shoot from start to finish. To break up one of my interviews only ruins the flow. Worse, in some cases, it forces some statements out of their natural context. If you're listening to part 11 of an interview, but the subject is referring to something based on a story he told in part 4, you can't help but be thrown off. It happens way too often with wrestlers as it is, and I simply refused to let that happen.

Edge and Christian

To this day, I regret taking so long to open up ClubWWI.com, especially because I had to cut a few very good interviews short. I spoke to Christian Cage, for example, during the week he became NWA Champion, and I had to end our talk abruptly. We'd gone long, and Cage had actually pulled into his driveway, parked his car, and continued speaking. Out of nowhere, I was like, "K. Bye." I remember hanging up and thinking, "Man, if only I could ask everything I wanted and not worry about the size of the file." It took me another seven months to figure out how to make that a reality. I'm sure Christian must have thought, *"What the hell?"*

Another problem the shows had was cursing. I don't mean small "c" cursing. Bitch, damn, ass . . . that's fine. I'm talking the F-bomb and every other expletive under the sun. Some people swear as part of their everyday speech — and wrestlers are even more colorful than many. I've never had the heart to ban swearing from the show; I've always wanted my guests to be themselves. If I asked guests not to curse, they'd be thinking more about watching their language than telling their story.

ClubWWI allowed me to let guests swear like sailors, while leaving me free to cut that stuff out of the weekly free shows that might be accessed by younger or more sensitive listeners. The full interview has it all; the edited RFI features clips safe for those who like their language G-rated.

At the same time, there are some people in the business who don't want to be associated with a show that allows foul language — after all, we're talking about the religious world of wrestling here. I'm not being sarcastic. Following a life of decadence, many stars turn to God to give them balance; they embrace God and live a life that follows strict guidelines. Part of that includes staying away from situations that promote potty talk. Consider the example of George "The Animal" Steele.

George "The Animal" Steele doing what he did best

I contacted George to be on episode 63. Most stars ask about past guests or how they can hear the show. Steele didn't. The man who never spoke an intelligible world through a long and successful career wanted to know about the language.

"Do you allow cursing on the interviews?" he asked when we first spoke.

"I don't curse — no."

I thought that might be a good way to dance around the question. In reality, I didn't . . . or at least not on the air.

"That's not what I mean. Do you allow the guests to curse?"

"Well, if someone has something to say, I don't censor them. We cut out the curses for our free show though." It made sense to me, but I could tell that I still felt he wasn't being specific enough.

"No, I mean, if you were to have the Iron Sheik on and he starts going off, do you stop him and tell him that cursing isn't allowed?"

Hmmm. Heck of a question. Iron Sheik . . . Iron Sheik . . . my memory's a bit hazy . . .

> "Otherwise I break his back! I fuck his ass! I make him to be humble because he's a no good punk, son of a bitch!"
> **— Iron Sheik (episode 22)**

"Ummm . . . I wouldn't let him curse during a WorldWrestling-Insanity.com interview. No . . ."

I wasn't lying. With the new setup, Sheik's rant would never be on the free show. With the old system, I had no choice. So, thanks to ClubWWI.com, we were able to welcome George "The Animal" Steele. I guess when you spend your green-tongued career eating turnbuckles, you want to make sure your golden years are free from potty mouth. It only makes sense. George was a real class act too; I was pleased to have him on as a guest and glad that the show's setup wouldn't interfere with his beliefs.

I get asked about editing interviews. Have I ever cut something out of a shoot before posting it? In other words, are there ever any mistakes?

Uh . . . yeah.

It doesn't happen often, but when it does, there's usually a pretty good reason for me to edit a piece. The first time it ever happened was during Dave Hebner's original "Radio Free Insanity" interview. I asked him a question and he began to answer — about halfway into his second word, he began to cough.

So I waited. And waited.

But he kept coughing. After that, he coughed a little more. It seemed to never end. Finally I had to ask if he was okay. He said he was, and we continued. For a brief moment, I feared Dave was going to croak during the interview, and that I'd have it on tape. Creepy.

Thankfully, he survived, and I simply cut around that part of the audio. Through the magic of computers, there was no problem fixing up the question so that it sounded like Hebner was swell . . . as if it never happened.

But it did happen, and it actually became a great way for me to explain the structure of the show to prospective guests. I ended up using Dave's coughing fit as an example. I would say, "The interview's prerecorded, so if anything comes up we can edit it out. For example, Dave Hebner had a massive coughing fit and I was able to cut it. So don't worry . . ."

I threw that in so wrestlers knew I wasn't insinuating they might tell me things and then later want to take them back — that I just meant call-waiting, nagging spouses, acts of God, coughing . . . you know, that kind of stuff.

I don't think I ever really said anything on air about it, though; it was just something I told guests to make them feel more at ease. But Jerry Lawler actually found the story really funny. It threw me off because most people don't even respond when I mention it. Jerry laughed, and even referenced it during his interview.

At one point in the discussion, Lawler let out a small cough. He followed with, "Oops, I'm having one of them Dave Hebner coughing fits."

I found it funny. I also thought I would get questions from listeners about it, but that didn't happen. While I'm sure many didn't even notice the comment, many of those who did probably assumed it was some backstage wrestling story that they should have known about anyway. . . .

It's not always what the guests have said that needs to be cut. While interviewing Paul Ellering, I naturally asked about the Road Warriors and their fighting style. I started off with "Let me ask you . . ."

Only it didn't come out like that. For some reason, my voice cracked. Big time. And I don't mean the kind of small, barely noticeable crack any self-respecting radio host might be a little self-conscious about. I mean a crack like Peter Brady singing with The Silver Platters kind of crack. Here I was, interviewing a guy who's "tough as a two dollar steak," to steal a phrase, and I sound like an eighth grader going through his awkward phase.

So yeah, I edited that out. If you pay close attention to the audio, you can tell. Only those who logged in and listened to this shoot during the very first hour it was online heard the full version. They're the lucky ones.

Unfortunately, not all bloopers are cracked voices. And believe me, that would be far less embarrassing. I admit it; I also cut around audio when something goes horribly awry. In the early days of Radio Free Insanity, something like that happened during an interview with the Phenomenal A.J. Styles. More than anything else, it serves as a lesson about how truly flawed the internet is. In preparation for A.J.'s shoot, I researched him online and discovered that he'd had an amazing ladder match with Eddie Guerrero during his early career. Eddie, who had just passed away, was someone every-body was talking about. I figured it would be great chance to ask Styles about fond memories.

"You had the chance to wrestle Eddie Guerrero in a ladder match. What were your memories . . . ?"

"I never wrestled Eddie Guerrero."

"Oh . . . I . . . Uh . . ."

"I guess I can't now."

"Yeah . . . I'll just cut that out."

The erroneous web reporting that plagues wrestling also lead me to ask Rodney Mack about "Gavin Archibald." A Wikipedia entry stated it was a name he once used. When I asked him about it, he laughed. I thought a story about some promoter would follow, that somebody thought he looked like his Uncle Gavin or something and turned it into a bad gimmick.

Nope. Rodney Mack laughed because he had no idea what the hell I was talking about.

That was 18 months after A.J.'s interview, and I should have already learned my lesson. This time, I didn't edit a thing, and instead transitioned into a question about poor internet reporting, asking Rodney about the craziest false story he'd ever heard about himself. It turned an embarrassing mistake on my part into a selling point. In the headline to his interview, I said that Rodney talked about the "Huge Error in His Wikipedia Entry." It sold better than saying: "James Guttman Asks a Completely Boneheaded Question!"

Another interview that got the shave-down treatment was Koko B. Ware. The Birdman was someone I'd wanted to speak with for a long, long time. Growing up with the WWF, I watched Koko as a kid, and I still remember searching high and low for the *Piledriver* album, the wrestling record on which he sang the title track. It was a quest that sent me, at the age of ten, on the suggestion of some-one at a local record store, to Home Depot. . . .

True story. It took them a while to figure out that I wasn't talk-ing about a tool. I felt like one though.

Koko was such a big part of my early days as a wrestling fan, I actually felt sorry for him when he didn't win the Slammy for song

Koko B. Ware

of the year in 1987. On some awards shows, artists lose out to other singers. But not the WWF's Slammys. Ware lost because Sika the Samoan ate the envelope that contained the winner's name. I guess no one remembered to write it down elsewhere. Poor Koko.

Anyway, everything was made right when I got to interview B. Ware. Almost right away, he told me that he still gets the urge to sing. With that, he broke into the chorus of "Piledriver." It was, and continues to be, one of my favorite moments. Hearing the guy who sang "Piledriver" actually sing it to me, on my show, was awesome.

That doesn't mean there weren't also some problems with this particular shoot. Like most guests, Koko made some contradictory statements. But it's not just wrestlers that this happens to — we'll all contradict ourselves if we talk long enough. And with interviews clocking in at 30 minutes or more, guys are sure to say controversial things that might not exactly jive with something else later. It's almost inevitable.

And Koko did exactly that. He was telling me about appearing in Barry Blaustein's widely released documentary, *Beyond the Mat*. The film, which at times demonstrated the harsh realities of professional wrestling, was famous for capturing Jake "The Snake" Roberts doing crack, and showing fellow ClubWWI.com guests Dennis Stamp and Terry Funk in what's become the famous "I'm Not Booked" scene. The flick also featured Ware, briefly, and it wasn't exactly complimentary.

In essence, Blaustein portrayed Koko as someone stuck in the past. They showed him in full Birdman garb, standing in his bedroom as he spoke about some wrestlers not being able to move on. It comes across harsh.

But guess what?

B. Ware doesn't care.

I asked him about it, and I didn't sugarcoat things. When I wondered how he felt about something that wasn't "the most positive piece in the world," he had this — admittedly, a bit confusing — to say . . .

> "I don't know what happens when these guys come in. That's why I'm so nervous now. I don't really do too much. Hey, you're not gonna use Koko B. Ware. If you're gonna use him, you gonna pay me for it. Because you pay everybody else. That's the thing with the camera. I don't mind doing the interview with you right now. . . . This is good for the people listening to it. I don't ask for an arm and leg, but if you guys want to donate something. I don't care. I'll take that. A little offer or whatever, but the thing is, you don't have to. Because it's free of charge."

You see that, right there, the ellipsis above?

There's a big chunk cut out. Right after "right now." You see, Koko had a whole digression that you didn't get to hear.

Why? Well, for starters, he said, "I want to help the little guy out. I want to help out your little show."

Great. Koko B. Ware just called my show little. The guy who sang Pile-friggin'-driver just did an anti-promo for "Radio Free Insanity." I thought about leaving it in anyway. What harm could it do? People would think that's funny, not a big deal, right? Ah, so many options to weigh . . .

As I began to ponder it all, he went on . . .

"Oh, oh . . . I don't know. I don't know. I don't mean to say you're little. You could be big . . . You can be the top-rated show on your radio station right now . . ."

That's when I stopped pondering and decided to cut the whole mess out. It's one thing when he says my show is small. It's another when confirms that he has no idea what the show even is.

All I needed now was for him to curse at me in Spanish and I'd have the best non-commercial for "Radio Free Insanity" ever!

Acts of God? Well, they've occurred too. In one case, the listeners were even let in on them. During Dr. Tom Prichard's last edition of "Tuesdays With Tom," we played some of them. Folks heard everything from pizza orders to near car crashes. Of course, because Dr. Tom was involved, most were followed up with "Daggonit!"

Ah, it isn't all embarrassing. Some bloopers and edited snippets are so much . . . fun.

This brings me, of course, to the infamous Ole Anderson shoot. Okay, maybe it was the flipside of fun. The insanity of my Afternoon With Ole will haunt me forever.

I still get e-mails from people telling me how sorry they felt for me.

Ole Anderson and Pat Patterson

Ole was . . . well, Ole.

A true proponent of everything old school, and a founding member of the Four Horsemen, Ole Anderson's known as a no-nonsense guy. Me? Well, I kind of like nonsense. Together, we were like mismatched roommates on the world's most insane reality show.

The thing that no one seems to get is that Ole was really nice when I originally set up the interview. He didn't take much convincing at all. Actually, he just asked me when I'd like to record, made some brief small talk, and agreed. I truly thought he'd be awesome on air. Ole Anderson was now my buddy.

Okay, to be honest, I didn't expect much when I called him the next day. Just some reminiscing about the olden days, and a few angry words for Eric Bischoff. No big whoop.

The focus of the interview was the WWE Four Horsemen DVD that had recently been released. Ole had been left out of the whole thing, and I figured I'd have the opportunity to glom onto the

DVD's success by interviewing the man they'd excluded. In essence, "Radio Free Insanity" would become a DVD extra. Thanks, WWE!

If you guys had only interviewed Ole Anderson, I wouldn't have had the chance to have him on — your loss.

I mean, why wouldn't you interview Ole? It makes no sense.

He was so nice to me . . .

When the interview began, I started with the question I now begin all the shoots with: "Why don't you let fans know what's going on by you and what's going on in the world of Ole Anderson right now?"

"Well, I can't give you anything that's really positive because I'm . . . uh, I'd be happy if I was dead. How's that?"

I expected him to follow that up with, "I'm only kidding! Waka-waka-waka!" So I laughed and said, "Ohhhhh-kay . . . ha, ha, ha."

"Yeah. I'm in bad health right now."

What the hell?

This guy just seriously told me that he wishes he was dead, and I answered by laughing in his face.

Great. We'd been talking for little more than a minute, and he probably already hated me.

"I'm different than when people watched me or whatever . . . I'm not the same."

Wow. Is this the same guy I spoke with just a day earlier?

I quickly also learned that Ole wasn't such a big fan of the Four Horsemen. Since the interview was set up primarily to talk about the DVD, I expected most of our discussion to revolve around that. Little did I know that Anderson considered that stage of his career to be "showbiz bullshit." Actually, I had no idea until, well, he told me that it was "showbiz bullshit."

He wanted to be remembered for his better contributions — but no one remembered, they just wanted to talk about the BS.

Even worse?

I was part of the problem.

"Unfortunately, people like yourself . . . when they think about the Andersons, Ole Anderson and Gene Anderson, the only thing they can come up with is the Four Horsemen, and that's unfortunate, because that, to me, was just a piece of crap. It was garbage."

I've found that whenever someone uses the phrase, "Unfortunately, people like yourself . . ." you're pretty much screwed. It's a polite way of saying, "You're a douche bag."

So, that's when the show went from bad to worse. To follow up, the former Minnesota Wrecking Crew member showed the whole world that I suck at math. He also confused the hell out of me, because I truly had no idea how we even got onto this subject. Basically, Ole set up his very own guessing game. Below, you'll find the unadulterated transcript. No names have been changed to protect . . . anyone.

Ole Anderson: Okay, well, I retired, and I . . . well, I'm gonna give you some more BS. A kid where I work out once in a while talked about how great he was when it comes to numbers. I said, 'Is that right?' and he says 'Oh yeah. When it comes to numbers, I know a lot about numbers. I know everything.' I said, 'Well, I'm not too bad with numbers.' He said, 'Well, you're not as good as I am.' I said, 'Well, let me give you an example of numbers that I can come up with. How much do you make an hour here?' The guy said he made six bucks an hour. I said, 'Okay. Here's what I know about numbers. You make six bucks an hour and I retired at 42.'

JG: How long would you have to work to retire at 42 making six bucks an hour?

OA: Well, he could never make it at 42. He could never make it at 82. He could never make it at any time. So, I made enough money to retire at 42. Now again, it becomes 'What the hell is enough money?' You know? So I ask you, what the hell do you think would be enough money? What would you consider to be enough money?

JG: Uh, well, it all depends on the time period.

OA: Oh, forget "time period." Time period, today, is now. The point I'm *trying* to make, which of course, at 30 years of age, you don't know what you're talking about anyway. And maybe you think I don't know what I'm talking about . . . probably. When I retired at the age of 42, that was 1984. Actually, before I was 42, I was 41 — but I count it 42. Um, it had to sustain me in 2007. This is the year now, 2007, isn't it?

JG: Yeah.

OA: So, when I retired in 1984, I had to have enough money to allow me to be able to retire, still be retired, in 2007. Does that make sense to you?

JG: No, that makes total sense. There's gotta be at least a couple of hundred thousand dollars.

At this point, we talked over each other until one of us got the floor. Guess who won?

OA: How much money would you have to have?

JG: Uh, I would, at least a couple of hundred thousand dollars, um . . .

OA: What would you do with a couple hundred thousand dollars?

JG: What would I do personally?

OA: Yeah.

JG: I mean, you could invest some, keep some, uh, you know, in savings, and things like that.

OA: How old are you again? 30?

JG: I'm 30.

OA: Okay. If you had, uh, two hundred thousand dollars and you were gonna retire on that, in 1984 . . .

JG: I didn't mean two hundred. I mean, at least five hundred thousand . . . five hundred, six hundred thousand dollars.

OA: Okay, make it six hundred thousand dollars. If you were going to retire in 1984 with six hundred thousand dollars in your pocket, you have a couple of choices. You could say, 'Well, I'm going to live for ten years,' so divide ten of the six hundred thousand, I'm gonna spend sixty thousand dollars a year. Or I could say, 'I'm gonna live 20 years,' and divide that into six hundred thousand dollars and say, 'Well, geez, I've only got thirty thousand dollars a year.' Well again, my mortgage payment is over twenty thousand, so that's . . . Well, gosh, I better have a lot more money than just six hundred thousand dollars. So I'm back to asking you, what do you think it would take for you to have, in 1984, to be able to retire and still be retired, in 2007, and tell people that offer you fifteen hundred bucks you don't need it? What would you have to have, do you think?

JG: Well now, just based on what you're telling me now, it's gotta be more than a couple of million, that you have there.

OA: Well, now you're getting closer. Now you're getting closer. Let's just say a couple of million. What are the interest rates right now? . . . You don't know.

JG: No.

OA: Well, let's just say safely somewhere around five percent. What's five percent of two million?

JG: Five percent of two million . . . shh, don't tell me.

OA: You'll need time to figure this one out.

JG: Yeah, we'll be here for a while, so you tell me.

OA: How about a hundred thousand?

JG: Okay.

OA: You go ahead and put your pencil down. I don't need a pencil. But anyway, now you go ahead and pay your taxes and so forth and so on, you might end up with forty or fifty or sixty thousand dollars, just depending on how you're taxed and everything else. Alright. Can you live on that? Yeah . . . yeah. So that's what you have . . . that's what you have to work toward, back in 1984. Does that make sense to you?

JG: It does; it does, actually. What's surprising is this, and this is why it's such a different kind of, uh, conversation . . .

OA: You don't know anybody like me, because there is nobody like me. . . .

Yeah, you got that right, Mr. Anderson.

Yikes.

I finally came to the conclusion that I should have just guessed as high as possible. The second he asked me how much money he made in order to retire, I should have said, "12 gazillion dollars!" It would have made the entire thing so much easier.

Okay, the thing is, I could have done all this . . . if I was prepared to do all this. I've never had a guest quiz me like Ole Anderson. It was nuts. He asked me how many nights he worked. He asked me how many people lived in Georgia back when he was wrestling. He asked me where Marietta was. It was like being on *Jeopardy*, with a pissed off and ornery Alex Trebek . . . and no prize money.

Not even a couple of hundred thousand dollars to retire on.

This is just about where we get to the part that was actually cut out of the broadcast. After all, things had been going so bad, they couldn't possible get worse . . . Right?

Wrong.

You see, I asked Ole if wrestling was different in his day because there was far less traveling, compared to today's wrestlers, in WWE.

For those of you taking notes: never ask Ole Anderson if wrestling was different in his day . . . because there was far less traveling, compared to today's wrestlers . . .

Before I explain what happened next, I should tell you more about my pre-interview routine. Essentially, I step away from my computer. Doing this prevents me from clicking around and searching the internet for questions during the discussion. I usually turn the computer off, but in this case I was burning a DVD.

During Ole Anderson's interview, I had the burner running hard. It virtually seized all my computer's memory in its quest to make me a great new Digital Video Disc. Remember this, because it's important.

Alright. So, Ole Anderson did not think WWE's wrestlers traveled more. In fact, he posited, they travel less! And although my interview style means I let guests speak, that I try not to engage in debate, I had no choice. The premise of my question was based upon a fact that Ole Anderson rejected completely.

Remember "Unfortunately, people like you"? This was the same thing. In other words, I'd pissed him off, again.

"Where are they right now? Where's WWE today?"

I had no idea. I knew where *I* was. That's all I really focused on. I told him I didn't know.

"You don't know? You're supposed to know."

I wasn't sure why, but I told him I could look it up. That was my way of saying, "Let's keep talking, and if you're still on this kick later, I can find out."

To Ole, it actually meant, "Hang on, I'll look it up."

An eerie silence was born. So, I went to my computer and tried to type in WWE's web address. But like I said, my computer was locked up. It was slower than you can even imagine — I'd have made better time running from Long Island to Titan Tower in Connecticut to ask the receptionist.

The silence grew louder.

"I'm waiting."

At this point, I realized I'd likely have to cut all of this out. It was ridiculous. The awkwardness stretched on and on. I didn't hear Ole even moving, not at all. I could picture him sitting in a chair with a phone on his ear and staring angrily, straight ahead. And then I imagined what he'd do to me if this were a face-to-face interview.

Okay, yeah . . . I should probably just cut this part out.

In an effort to retain some dignity, I tried to explain what was going on.

"Sorry. The computer's slow."

"So's the guy using it."

That's when I decided that I was definitely cutting this stuff out.

I kept my cool because, well, why not? To be perfectly blunt, I really couldn't care less whether Ole Anderson likes me. I'm sure he feels the same way. I'm not saying this just because of him — it's not personal. I feel the same way about almost every guest. We don't have to share a Sanka and cry during *Titanic;* we just have to co-exist for a brief interview.

Then again, with our chemistry, I'm sure we'd make a great buddy cop movie. We'd fight crime and save Marietta from the evil forces of Math.

I suppose that was Ole being Ole. That's the old saying, after all. Isn't it? "That's just Ole being Ole." I get what it means now. Big time.

As this bit of insanity mercifully came to a close, I asked Anderson if he used e-mail. It's something I usually ask after an interview ends. When a guest says yes, I set them up with a free ClubWWI account.

This time, of course, I felt like a complete idiot the second the words were out of my mouth.

"What? No. You don't have to give me nothing."

"Alright . . . Thanks again, Ole. It was great getting to talk to you."

Click.

So, Ole Anderson thought I was part of the problem. And what problem is that?

The "everyone sucks and only cares about the Horsemen" problem, that's what. That doesn't mean I don't try to do some good for wrestling when I can.

I should have told Ole to ask Demolition . . .

CHAPTER SIX

. . . BUT YOU CAN'T TAKE PRO WRESTLING OUT OF THE WRESTLER

One of the best things about running the sites is that occasionally I can help a performer. When I get the opportunity to offer assistance to someone I've watched wrestle, it means a lot to me.

Over the course of their existence, World Wrestling Insanity and ClubWWI have presented both audio hosts and columnists from the wrestling industry. Even though they were unpaid, people like D-Lo Brown, Bull Buchanan, Lisa Moretti, Orlando Jordan, Kevin Kelly, and Dr. Tom Prichard all willingly took part in the Insanity. There's no way I'll ever be able to show them enough appreciation.

And here's the coolest thing. They appreciated it too. It blows my mind still, realizing that these big names enjoy working with us as much as they do. The most common reason they're happy to oblige? It's an uncomplicated outlet, the chance for them to speak their minds on the wrestling industry and reach out to fans. It keeps them front and center and allows them to tell readers and listeners that there's more to them than what was on television.

Aside from introducing me to some truly kooky personalities, running these sites has also given me the opportunity to right some wrongs. One of these first became apparent to me when I was just 15.

I grew up in Lindenhurst, New York. The town is tiny, but for some inexplicable reason it has nine 7-Elevens. Pat Benatar and the dad from *Wonder Years* are from Lindenhurst. . . . So yeah, you probably haven't heard much about it.

Wrestling never came to Lindy. That's what the cool people call it — Lindy. There was one WWF card, sure, at the high school, in 1987: it featured Bob Orton, The Hart Foundation, Kamala, and some others. No, Lindy didn't get much local auditorium rasslin'.

Babylon, though, that was another story.

I don't mean the biblical Babylon. I mean Babylon, New York, the next town over. Their high school hosted more wrestling than ours could ever dream about. One of the few shows I went to was a 1992 showcase of World Wrestling Superstars.

Before I say anything else, let me tell you, it was great. I sat in the second row and couldn't believe the difference between this show and the one the WWF put on at my town's high school years earlier. The heckled wrestlers yelled back. The referee would try to explain why he missed the bad guy's cheating. You were practically in the ring.

Sure, the show had some unknown guys. Don Rock? Kodiak Bear? Not really sure what they're up to now, but they were with me in Babylon. There were others I'd never heard of, but Don and Kodiak are the ones who really stuck with me. They weren't the only stars though . . .

We saw former big name talent who had left their home companies to slum with us high school gym-rats. S.D. Jones grappled. Jimmy Snuka took on Hercules Hernandez in the main event. But the biggest deal of all? Demolition!

Demo-friggin'-lition, baby! The monsters who dominated WWF's tag scene for forever and a half — two of the scariest tag team competitors to ever lace up a pair of spiked leather masks! In Babylon! My hometown! Well, next to my hometown . . . but close enough! Sweet! That's right. Here comes the Ax and here comes the . . .

Blast?

Who the hell is Blast? It's Smash, stupid. *Smash.* Smash is Ax's partner. Without Smash, there's no one to threaten to kick your stinkin' teeth down your throat. There's no voice of reason . . . no ying to the yang. There's no Demolition.

This wasn't Demolition. It was half of Demolition and . . . *Blast.* It's like when Axl Rose put the KFC bucket on that guy's head and tried to call it Guns N' Roses. What the hell? Demolition is Ax and Smash.

Under the greasepaint, Ax was Bill Eadie and Smash was Barry

Darsow. Not only were they both famous for their run with this team, they're also famous for being part of many other important tag teams, gimmicks, and angles. Bill originally achieved fame as The Masked Superstar and later became a part of the great Japanese team known as the Machines. He even got to get beat up by Hulk Hogan in the opening minutes to the epic film, *No Holds Barred*. He was Bolo Mongol! Bill Eadie was much more than just the Ax . . .

Demolition: Ax and Smash

And Barry Darsow was much more than the Smasher. In fact, when I first thought to call him for an interview, I didn't know what I would put on his interview-hyping banner. I mean, we're talking about the Repo Man. WWF's answer to . . . well, repo men. Wearing a lone ranger mask, he would steal cars and take them away from deadbeats. The gimmick was insane, but awesome. The same can be said for his other incarnations. Krusher Kruschev, Hole in One, Blacktop Bully . . . okay, maybe not Blacktop Bully.

Anyway, I'd had Bill Eadie's phone number for a while, but just never got around to calling him. I felt like there was something missing, you know? The idea of speaking with just him somehow didn't seem . . . complete. Would I bill the thing as an interview with the "Masked Superstar" Bill Eadie? That didn't make much sense, considering that the Superstar was a bit before my time and Demolition Ax was someone I grew up with. But what could I do? Try to hype an interview with just half of Demolition?

And no, I was not planning on calling in Blast, wise guy.

I set out to find Barry Darsow. I went through a couple of different channels and even spoke to his mother at one point. In the end, we caught up with each other and we were good to go. Before we began, I explained what I was thinking.

The plan was to present a two-part show. One half — Eadie. The other half — Darsow. I told Barry about this and, knowing that they hadn't been together for the better part of two decades, waited to see if he'd balk. He didn't.

Darsow seemed happy to hear my idea and explained that he harbored no ill will toward Eadie. He was eager to do the interview. At the end of our discussion, live and on air, he asked me to pass along his info to Ax.

"Listen, tell Bill Eadie I said hi. Give him my number and tell him I'd love to get together with him, have a beer, and just laugh."

It was great to hear. I felt halfway home. Anyway, next up was Demolition Ax.

Now, keep in mind, I had no idea what led to the rift between these guys. For all I know, Barry may have killed Bill's pet. I still hadn't even spoken to Eadie about appearing with Darsow, and I wasn't sure he'd be okay with the concept. Besides, if you ever saw these two behemoths on TV, you know Ax always seemed a bit . . . scarier. His low, gravelly voice could frighten the Hulkamania bandanna right off your head.

When I reached Eadie, he sounded remarkably like the terrifying man I remembered, maybe a little bit softer. I mustered the nerve to tell him I'd interviewed Barry and . . . he was good with it. I said that Darsow had asked that I pass along his number and he wrote it down. Things were set . . . Demolition would be reunited — on my show!

That's when Bill asked if he could get back to me in three weeks because he was going on vacation.

A bit flustered, I asked when he was leaving. Tomorrow? The day after?

"Right now. My wife and I are holding our luggage."

At that point, I almost fell down. With one half of my master plan already complete, I didn't want to wait three weeks. The whole thing would be thrown out of sync somehow. Time-wise, waiting for almost a month, the immediacy of the exchange would be messed up.

I explained this to Bill and, in a testament to the kind of person he is, he stopped everything to do the interview. He delayed leaving for a vacation with his wife so that he could speak to my listeners. It meant a hell of a lot to me; I gained a whole new level of respect for the man.

Today, the real Demolition is back. Ax and Smash are together once more, tearing up wrestling conventions and indie shows, and making other appearances. Finally, after way too long, fans can interact with the duo that ruled the WWF back in the day.

Honestly? I like to think that they would have eventually gotten back together on their own. Maybe Barry would have run into Bill at the movies or something — okay, that would have been weird, since they live in different states. I'm proud to think that I may have played a small part in making it all happen . . . sooner. Because of our interviews people will never again be subjected to the bizzaro version of Demolition I saw in Babylon.

Another wrestler I was thrilled to see enjoy a renaissance after his ClubWWI interview was Damien Demento. It was like the guy used the appearance to springboard back into the collective consciousness of wrestling fans and prove he could still work the crowd like the best of them.

Growing up in the Northeast, I heard a lot about some of wrestling's future stars before they made it. Guys like Tazz, Tommy Dreamer, The Sandman, Cactus Jack, and others all worked hard in this area before they became household names. Two of my favorites from the hardcore indie scene were D.C. Drake and Mondo Kleen. One of them made it to the big show, the other . . . didn't.

Mondo's the guy who made it. For those who never saw him perform, Mondo Kleen was insane. He had big furry shoulder pads and a goatee that nearly reached his bellybutton. He looked . . . freaky. When the WWF eventually picked him up, they renamed him "Damien Demento" but left the rest of his gimmick untouched.

Damien Demento main-evented the first *Raw*. That's a big deal. On episode one The Undertaker battled Damien in the feature. No matter what else Demento would do in his WWF stint, it would always be the biggest moment — a pretty huge feather in his furry shoulder pads.

Shortly after that milestone, Damien seemed to disappear. Back to the "Outer Reaches of Your Mind" — his purported hometown — I suppose. How in the world was I gonna find a guy who lives in my mind?

Thankfully, there's a crazy little thing called Google.

I started my search: where was Damien Demento, or rather Phil Theis, the man who played him? Why had he dropped out of sight? Why couldn't I find anything about his current situation?

And then Google led me to YouTube. Someone named "TheOriginalDemento" had been posting. He was an artist from New York, and he had a number of videos online. Chomping on a cigar, the Original One would showcase his artwork and explain his inspiration for each piece. Most of his works were sculptures made from common items. It was actually really impressive to see and learn about what the guy was doing. He took pride in his work and wasn't really looking to sell anything. He just wanted to show what he'd created. It was cool.

I was also sure it was the real Damien Demento.

It looked like him. It sounded like him. More importantly, it was someone claiming to be him, without looking to make a buck. He had to be the real deal.

I registered for a YouTube account just so I could e-mail him, then I sent out a letter of introduction and waited. I wasn't holding my breath. Demento hadn't done anything wrestling-related for almost a decade. I was thinking he'd probably just turn me down. After all, I couldn't be the only one looking for him, and asking him for an interview, right?

Apparently, I was. When Phil Theis wrote back to me, he asked about the kinds of questions I wanted to pose, so I sent him a list outlining what I'd like to discuss. We exchanged a few e-mails, and when we finally spoke, I was shocked.

Why? Well, one of the things I check with most guests is whether or not they've done other shoot interviews since leaving the last company they were with. People like Al Snow, Jazz, Rob Conway, Sylvan Grenier, Orlando Jordan, Ron Killings, and many others have all done their first shoots with ClubWWI after their WWE or TNA run. Some of the most excited moments in the show's history have come from guests who have yet to have the opportunity to speak to fans as themselves.

Phil Theis, however, took the show to a whole new level. My interview would be his first shoot *ever*. That's right. Despite being in the wrestling business for many years, main-eventing the first *Raw*, and appearing with some of the industry's most well-known talent, Phil had never done a shoot. Not one.

Phil would be talking to fans "straight-up" for the first time. It would be the debut of the man they called Demento.

Here's the thing with Damien: he has a great mind for wrestling. Even after being out of the business for years, he can still get a rise out of the fans, particularly with his answer to my "Who do you wish you could have worked with" question. As you'll see later on in this book, even in the early '90s, Demento wanted to work the people. And that's precisely what he did following our interview.

Soon after our shoot, I was told to check out Phil's YouTube presence — his account had been inundated with new subscribers. Many were — as wrestling fans can quite often be — um, blunt. It's a bizarre trend I've noticed in wrestling's audience, and I some-times despair it's become the norm. They were calling Demento all kinds of names, and hoping he'd respond.

At first I didn't get that kind of mentality. I've heard stories of fans cursing out a wrestler on MySpace, only to develop doting crushes when the wrestler writes back. Yeah, it's bizarre, but in a nutshell, it sounds like a lot of people follow the credo that says the squeaky wheel gets the grease. But I'm here to tell you, you don't have to piss off a rassler to get a response. You just need patience and tact.

In the case of Demento, however? Don't worry about it. Forget tact and manners, go off on the guy. It gets to him — or so it seemed.

His YouTube videos, once a quiet and happy journey into the world of his art, quickly became angry rants against those who called him a "jobber" — the worst insult you can level at a wrestler (just ask Skull Von Kruss). He threatened to ban these people, and to close his YouTube account. According to Damien Demento, he "didn't ask for this."

To be honest, I felt bad . . . for a few minutes. Then I remembered his fondness for working wrestling fans. As time passed, the rants continued and his name, previously unuttered for more than a decade, magically returned to wrestling's headlines. I thought it was pretty great.

Shortly thereafter, I heard about Phil doing a wrestling convention — and I couldn't help but smile. A new generation of fans would have the chance to meet Mondo Kleen. I was pleased to play a small part in this, and even happier that Damien Demento was once more working the people.

There have been other similar instances in our history. In December 2006, I interviewed "The Doctor of Style" Slick, a former WWF manager who had seemingly fallen off the edge of the Earth. After years away from the spotlight, the Slickster announced on my show that he was accepting bookings again. I figured he might appear in a TNA skit or something.

Four months later, he had a cameo at *WrestleMania*.

Sometimes the good that comes with doing an interview is in simply doing the interview. It's about allowing someone to explain past actions or show their current passion for the wrestling business.

I see my interview with Tony "Ahmed Johnson" Norris as one of the best examples of this. Ahmed, one of WWF's biggest stars in the mid-'90s, had become the first African-American Intercontinental Champ. Then, one day, he was gone. The man from Pearl River simply left Monday Night *Raw* and never explained why. According to many articles, he took issue with an angle the company proposed to him. When I finally caught up with him for an interview, however, he revealed the truth. It was something that, more than a decade later, he had still not told Vince McMahon.

"When I left, the reason I did leave — and the reason I didn't tell Vince is because I'm not a crybaby — is that my sister was dying. And she died, like, three days after I walked out the door. And they didn't know I was dealing with that, you know?"

As Johnson spoke about his sister's battle with cancer and his decision to not tell McMahon, everything became clear. This was a tough-as-nails superstar who had been a member of the Bloods. (It's why he wore red in the ring.) I mean, he played Suge Knight in the MC Hammer story. You don't get more badass than Ahmed Johnson. Considering his past, his entire demeanor, it made sense that he wouldn't tell McMahon.

To many fans, however, his sudden departure and the lack of an explanation meant that he was a "prima donna." Johnson addressed that with me. His unwillingness to speak about his personal issues at the time was based on pride, on not wanting to seem like he was exploiting a family tragedy for sympathy. It was never because he was angry with the company. This truly moved me and I was happy to give him a forum where he could clear the air. And even though Vince McMahon himself may never tune in to hear it, at least it's out there. Perhaps someone could let him know?

As we delved deeper and started to reveal some of Johnson's real feelings, he blew me away by saying, "It was killing me for a while. It was even killing me to the point where I was thinking about committing suicide . . . You know? And I never told anybody that. You're the first person I ever told that to . . . except for a friend of mine. You're the only person I ever told that to in an interview."

When Ahmed, or Tony Norris rather, said that, I did not think about the sensation it would cause, press releases never crossed my mind. I thought about how I had succeeded in creating the kind of warm environment where wrestlers could feel comfortable in speaking out. Imagine what it meant to me, that a guy as tough as Tony, so guarded that he didn't even tell his boss he was quitting because his sister was dying, felt comfortable enough to share all this with me. I was glad that I was able to offer him the chance to get it off his chest.

As I've said, there are as many different personalities in wrestling as there are wrestlers. Much like Tony, Shawn Stasiak spoke candidly on the show. In fact, he admitted something that many others would be more than apprehensive to admit. It speaks a lot about the person he is, and about the honesty of his shoot: "What really inspired me to even consider thinking about making a return was when I watched the WWE Hall of Fame . . . I cry most of the times I watch it. Okay? I cry because I saw Roddy Piper and I saw Paul "Mr. Wonderful" Orndorff, you know? Whoever. Mean Gene. All these guys . . . Bret Hart. Steve Austin. All the guys who get inducted . . . like Jack Lanza . . . All these guys that I see that are being inducted are all people — a lot of them are from my dad's era, and that brings me closer to him."

Stasiak was a fascinating guest. He'd been out of the business for a while and working as a chiropractor. And while fans may remember him as Meat or Planet Stasiak, he knew himself as Stan Stasiak's son.

Stan "The Man" Stasiak was WWWF Champion back in the 1970s and, until Andre the Giant "surrrrr-endered the Wordheabbywait champeensheep to Ted DiBiase" in 1988, he held the record for the company's shortest reign, holding the strap for nine days.

But nine days in the 1970s wasn't the same as nine days in the '90s, or post-Y2K. Back then, titles were true titles. There wasn't a new champion every week. When you won that belt, you'd achieved something. Say what you want about the duration of Stan's time on top, but it *was* a big deal. He beat Pedro Morales, and when he lost, it was to WWWF icon Bruno Sammartino. In the grand scheme of all things wrestling, that's nothing to sneeze at.

Shawn Stasiak is a rarity in the wrestling industry — he wasn't doing it for money, he wasn't doing it for fame. He was doing it for his dad. His entire interview convinced me of that.

Now before you jump up and down with your bad cynical selves and say he's just putting out some good PR, hear me out. You could tell that he was wrestling for his dad, who passed away when Shawn

Shawn Stasiak shows Pedro Morales and Bruno Sammartino his father's famous heart punch

was still young, because of how he spoke about the man. Any father listening to the interview can only hope that his son or daughter would one day hold him in as such high esteem.

In the way Stasiak spoke, it was clear he was also upset with himself. Shawn has a history of backstage heat. Plagued by rumors of secretly recording conversations with wrestlers while he was with WWF, he's constantly being looked at with suspicion.

What's with this kid? Is he crazy? The man who majored in communications in college, explained:

> "I just love production, you know? I want to be in front of the camera, behind the camera. It's just the way I've been and anyone who knows me as Shawn knows that there was absolutely no harmful intent whatsoever. . . . I was in a car with a couple of folks and I was just recording without their knowledge. We were in Montreal or somewhere. Tired and irritable and everything's in French. We were hungry and looking for directions. We were lost. They were bitching and complaining and fighting,

you know, in a fun-loving way. But I just thought it would be funny to record and play it back for them later, but then — long story short — I was approached by one of them and he was concerned about it . . . that I was recording and I just — where I went wrong is I lied."

Well, the whole story sounded more innocent coming from Shawn's mouth . . . and telling it also gave him a chance to take responsibility for mistakes he made when he was younger. He accepted and shouldered the blame for what he'd done, and expressed real regret over the way he handled the situation. Anyone over the age of 25 has to feel for him.

Think of the insane stuff you did in your late teens or early 20s. Go ahead. Think. I'll wait. . . .

Oh my. Bad, right? Pushed some of that stuff to the back of your brain, huh?

Well, that's what happened to Shawn Stasiak. Years later, and much more mature, the former Planet had realized the error he made and wanted desperately to have a shot making things right.

Admitting to crying during Hall of Fame ceremonies was a brave revelation in a shoot interview, a raw, emotional moment in which he exposed himself to wrestling's fans.

I was dumbstruck by what it meant. Some former WWE guys don't even watch the show any more. You ask, "You still watch *Raw?*" They go, *"Hell no!"* Stasiak not only watches the shows, he's emotionally connected to them.

In our interview he made his case for why WWE or TNA should sign him. He even presented some storyline ideas about how his character could be reality-based and feature a son paying tribute to his father. As I write this, he still hasn't been signed.

That's a real shame. In a business where guys get massive pushes only to later give the industry the middle finger, Shawn Stasiak is someone who has the kind of heart promoters worldwide look for. He's connected to the industry through his respect for his father. Plus now, years of maturity have given him perspective: he's learned what it means to be out of the spotlight and would clearly work harder than he ever did before.

I'd sign him in a heartbeat for that reason alone.

The admission of past mistakes has become a big part of many interviews. And I guess you could say it's also a big part of why these kinds of interviews even exist. Thanks to ClubWWI, fans have heard people like Al Snow take responsibility for his bitterness in the early stages of his career, or BG James regret a past that included drug abuse — they've even heard Nick "Eugene" Dinsmore explain why WWE terminated his contract. It's a chance for stars to set the record straight, to tell the world not only their side of the story, but also update the world about who they are today because of their struggles. In some cases, stars have been able to show all the doubting Thomases out there in fandom that they've truly come full circle.

It also allows some of them to make surprising revelations about themselves. The former "Masterpiece" Chris Masters is just one example. He appeared shortly after departing from WWE. Chris, a muscular youngster, with a Lex Luger-esque gimmick, had been stigmatized as a bodybuilder turned wrestler. Like a lot of people, I too believed this was a fact, set in stone. Wrestling must have been his fallback position, when bodybuilding didn't work out, right?

Chris Masters and Nick "Eugene" Dinsmore

Nope. That couldn't be further from the truth.

My discussion with Masters (now known as Mordetzky) set everything I thought I knew about him on its ear. He loved the wrestling industry. He knew its history and had followed it long before he ever debuted. According to the misunderstood man himself, he may have been a bodybuilder turned wrestler, but that's because he started bodybuilding . . . in *anticipation* of a wrestling career.

That makes more sense, doesn't it? Especially when you consider that he continues to wrestle today. Leaving WWE didn't send him scurrying into bodybuilding competitions.

One of the craziest things about Masters' shoot was that the WWE's *Smackdown* vs. *Raw* 2008 video game had just come out that week. Now I don't pretend to be anything but what I truly am — a fan of wrestling — so I admit I had the game in my PlayStation 2 that week. I'd picked it up a few days before the interview and I was already hooked.

Actually, I was deeply immersed in what would turn out to be a disappointing "General Manager" mode. In essence, I was taking my computerized superstar to the top of WWE through what was essentially a season. You had to face different opponents and were on a quest to win different titles. At the time I conducted this interview, my game was paused. My wrestler was feuding with — you guessed it — Chris Masters.

This was definitely one of those times where it helps to be able to differentiate a wrestler's persona from who he is in real life. It took a lot of effort for me not to say, "Yo, Masterpiece, why the hell did you attack me after our tag match?"

Discovering who stars really are is just about the best part of what I get to do. And in doing this, I've had the opportunity to meet some pretty, um, *big* personalities.

Holla if you hear me.

CHAPTER SEVEN

EXCEEDING EXPECTATIONS

Scott Steiner is awesome.

I've always thought that. Way back when, I was a fan of the All-American Scott, the guy with the wavy mullet who blew my mind with his Frankensteiner. When he became the Big Bad Booty Daddy, the guy with the tri-color goatee and who cut promos about giving women the "Big O," well, I became even more of a fan. Yeah, it's simple: Scott Steiner is awesome.

The thing about Steiner that makes him really stand out is how far he veered from his original gimmick. Very few wrestlers are able to successfully transition into such a radically different character and succeed. Steiner doesn't even look like the same person. If it wasn't for the fact that early '90s Scott occasionally spoke, I wouldn't believe they were the same guy. I'd think today's Freakzilla was some distant Steiner relation.

Beyond this, there was one other thing I *thought* I knew about Scott Steiner. He was crazy. I mean, you read some of the stories about him and that seems likely. After all, the guy's arms are the size of my garage. He's nothing if not an intimidating dude.

I scheduled Scott's interview with the TNA office. He was supposed to phone me at 1 p.m.

He never called.

I wasn't surprised. Steiner isn't the kind of guy who does lots of these interviews. I figured I'd just schedule someone else. I wrote it off.

Around 5, my phone rang. I answered.

"James."

"Yes?"

"Scott Steiner."

In the same voice that had done so many memorable promos, he told me he was given my number and that he was supposed to do an interview. I couldn't believe that I was hearing Scott Steiner on my phone. I also couldn't believe that he made small talk in the same frightening, gravely tone he used to threaten opponents with dismemberment.

"What kinda questions you wanna ask me?"

Okay, that was a dilemma in itself. Who knew what he did or didn't want to talk about? I couldn't very well lie to him now, lobbing softball questions at him, and then ask something controversial when we were recording. Garage arms, remember?

I decided to be straight up with him. We'd talk about his recent WWE run, his feud with Triple H, why it didn't go well, Ric Flair, the Frankensteiner, and stuff like that. I figured he was going to tell me to stick it and hang up.

There was a brief pause.

"Okay. When you wanna do this?"

I was amazed. I was almost positive he'd blow me off. Instead, we agreed on a time and day. It was all set. Before we hung up, I said, "Holla if you hear me!"

No. I didn't.

I thought it though.

A few days later, I called Steiner and the interview was underway. I can't even begin to explain how great it truly was. Scott tore into Triple H, Ric Flair, Shawn Michaels — and anyone else he felt had it coming — with reckless abandon. Unflinching, unapologetic, and completely in-your-face, Steiner let it all hang out. It was one of the best interviews anyone's ever given.

I wish you could have heard it.

Yup, you read that right. Read what follows, and try to put yourself in my position. Talk about nearly puking your heart up.

I had just finished interviewing Big Poppa Pump. My major coup, an interview with a former WCW Champion who almost never did interviews, was now complete. All I had to do now was post it online. Except . . . when I looked down, there was no red light.

You're probably saying, "Huh? Red light?"

Yes. Red light.

The red *recording* light.

Holy crap. What do you think ran through my head? My initial thought was, "I'm screwed. I'm not calling this guy back. He's going to come here and kill me."

After all, that's what everyone says about him, right? Scott's crazy and he kills people. While he was cordial on the phone, I could only imagine the ire that was about to come down on me for daring to ask him to do it all over again.

But then I thought about the show. . . . I really wanted this interview and, at the end of the day, it's all about bringing the readers and listeners of World Wrestling Insanity the best I possibly can. In this particular instance, I had already managed to get just that. Now, I just needed to muster up the courage to do it a second time.

I picked up the phone and prepared to meet my maker. I mean, this wasn't a five-minute chat that didn't record . . . we're talking 45-minutes of Scott Steiner's life. I had wasted nearly an hour of his time, and now I was calling to ask for more. Even a somewhat-nice person would tell me to beat it in a heartbeat. Considering Steiner's rep, I clocked my chances at somewhere between zero and none.

When Scott answered the phone, I said hello and hurriedly explained the situation. I closed my eyes and braced for the worst.

"When you want to do it again? How about Monday?"

I was about to begin pleading for my life when I suddenly realized he had just agreed. Had I really heard him correctly?

According to many reporters, Scotty is one of the most volatile people in wrestling. Something like this should have sent him into a rage.

Uh uh. He was awesome. Just like I told you at the start of this chapter.

I'm not trying to destroy Big Poppa Pump's reputation here by telling the world that he's a nice person — but it's the truth. He's one of the most professional people I've ever dealt with when setting up an interview, and probably the most accommodating considering the extenuating circumstances. I can't think of many others who would have agreed to a do-over as quickly and readily as Steiner.

The second interview wound up being even better than the first. Scott hit all the high points, and once again no one was safe. What struck me most about Scotty's critiques of other stars was that he wasn't mean-spirited or angry in his delivery. If anything, Steiner spoke about people he didn't like in a matter-of-fact way. He didn't call people names to be mean or just to laugh at them. He called then names because, well, he considered them to be what he just called them.

> "Just look at [Shawn Michaels], look at his career. He comes out with chaps, black-leather chaps. Dance like a faggot, little Chippendale, and poses for a fag magazine . . . *Playgirl*. I mean, come on. It's a joke. . . . The Rock didn't want to wrestle him at *WrestleMania*. I mean, a lot of people don't like Shawn Michaels. He's a cocky little bastard, you know. Actually, he's one of those guys who would talk, and then, you know, when push comes to shove . . . Ask Ron and Don Harris. They grabbed him by the goozle and lifted him up and tears came out his eyes. They threw him down. I couldn't believe he was crying after being such a cocky little shit, you know? . . .
>
> "Hunter is the male version of a blonde bitch going to Hollywood and fucking her way up to the top. . . . He's basically the Kevin Federline of professional wrestling. If it wasn't for who he was married to, or all his skeezin' all over the place, he wouldn't be in this business. I mean, look where he started. He actually started in WCW, as Terra Ryzin. And then he was doing 30-second jobs for the Ultimate Warrior. All of a sudden he starts banging the boss's daughter and, all of a sudden, he's supposed to be the baddest man on the planet? I mean, come on . . . It's a joke. I don't think anyone else would say any different . . . I mean, that's my view, but there's guys in merchandising . . . guys behind the camera, they used to say the same shit. But they gotta watch what they say, you know, because everybody's in fear for their life."

Yeah, there's only one Scott Steiner. And it's statements like these that have shaped the public's perception of the Big Bad Booty Daddy. I had the chance to learn that there's much more to him than what some whisper about behind the scenes, and for that I'm grateful. He's a real stand-up guy.

A few months later, I interviewed his brother, Rick. When he asked me what Scott had to say, I read him those very same quotes.

The Steiner Brothers

Rick laughed in a way that told me he'd heard it all before, and replied, "That's Scotty alright. I'm going to give you something a bit different, though."

The Steiner Brothers are just two of the stars I was thrilled to finally speak with personally. Another I watched as a kid, watched as a teenager — hell, I just watched him last week — is the true King of Wrestling, Jerry Lawler.

Over the years, I've heard a lot about Lawler. Opinions about The King vary as greatly as opinions on Vince McMahon. Some people, like Al Snow, loved him — Al called him the greatest worker ever. Of all time.

That's big.

Others, well, they have their opinions, too.

Kevin Kelly? Not a big fan.

In my opinion, Lawler is a true great. The thing I loved about him was that he wasn't just hilarious — he could be completely and deadly serious at the drop of a hat. You never knew what you were going to get from the King.

This is the man who made David Letterman's audience laugh when he asked Andy Kaufman, "What kind of guy are you?" Ten seconds later he elicited shocked gasps when he slapped Kaufman so hard he knocked him to the floor.

Shifting from funny to serious at the drop of a hat is tough to pull off. Others in the business have been able to play comedy and drama, but few have been able to do both at once and be effective. To me, that puts Lawler on his own plane. And even without this ability he'd still rate high in my books; I mean, over the years, he's one of the few performers who have ever made me laugh out loud during televised wrestling.

One of my top King moments took place during one of my all-time favorite WWE feuds. It occurred when "Big Show" Paul Wight faced off with Big Bossman. The premise? Big Show's dad had cancer. Bossman began mocking him, and then exposed Show's illegitimacy by secretly taping his mother's confession. It was, simply, bizarre; the feud eventually led to Paul riding on top of his dad's coffin across a cemetery while Bossman towed it with his cop car. Okay, so I guess you had to be there. . . .

(A small side note is in order here. Think about it. One day that angle will be considered "old school." In the future grizzled veterans will complain to youngsters, "No one rides coffins or does necrophilia angles anymore! What's happened to *real* rasslin'?")

Anyway, Jim Ross, Jerry Lawler's long-time announcing partner, always talked about Big Show's "Daddy." J.R., with his drawl, made it sound natural. It was like Opie calling his dad "Pa." Must be an Oklahoma thing.

I became used to it. Ross said it every week. "Big Show's Daddy, King! That's Big Show's Daddy!" After a few weeks of this, J.R. said it again, during a match. That's when Lawler, in a matter-of-fact way, said: "Big Show's Daddy? Daddy? Come on. It's his father. Grow up, J.R."

I laughed out loud, and I'll never forget it. It was, and is, so funny because it came out of nowhere. Jerry's timing and delivery were perfect.

In March 2007, I was given Jerry Lawler's number. I had been looking for a way to contact him for an interview — it had just been announced that he'd be inducted into WWE's Hall of Fame. I figured I might never get a better opportunity to speak with him. Of course, when you run a site that's called World Wrestling Insanity, getting the co-host of World Wrestling Entertainment's top show to appear is at best a long shot. . . .

That's not the only reason I wasn't expecting much when I dialed up Lawler. I simply didn't think he'd answer. I should have known better: all of the interviews that most would consider my biggest happened within a day of when I called for the first time. Kevin Nash, Eric Bischoff, Mae Young, DDP — they all agreed right away. It's the interviews you'd never expect to take weeks to set up that inevitably do. Guys like Lawler, for some reason, do it right away or not at all. So I wasn't exactly prepared when the King answered and booked me for the following day.

The next day was a Tuesday; I called when I said I would, half-expecting to get no answer. Jerry picked up. He was surprised, though. Lawler believed we'd be speaking in a week's time. I immediately panicked.

My first thought was that we'd hang up after agreeing to speak in a week, and that he'd then promptly forget, or that I'd never reach him again. That happens too, more than you'd think. I've had people say, "Call me in four days;" only when I call back, their number's been disconnected or they've moved to Cuba. Weird stuff . . .

Before I could even begin to give him my best telemarketing rebuttals, Lawler proved he wasn't brushing me off: "Alright. Tell you what . . . call me in an hour. I'm just waiting on a motorcycle delivery."

Okay, we're good to go. It was going to happen, no problem. If his phone's disconnected in the next hour or he buys a house in Cuba, more power to him.

No, that's not what happened. When I called an hour later, Jerry was eating his breakfast. We spoke for a bit, and then I got to listen to him eat. It's true. After explaining the site and how interviews were posted . . . I waited while he ate. And surprisingly, it was funnier than you'd think.

"Mmmm . . ." Chomp, chomp, chomp. "Almost done." Chomp, chomp, chomp. "One more bite." Chomp. Chomp. "One more after that." Hee-hee! Chomp. Chomp. "Wait . . . hang on. One more." Chomp.

While Jerry chomped, all I could think was: I'm on the phone with Jerry Lawler and he's eating breakfast. If I could travel back in

Jerry Lawler and Jimmy Hart in Memphis

time to tell myself at 15 that this would be happening to me at 30, I'd flip the hell out.

When the interview finally began, Jerry was phenomenal. He even produced a sound bite that I'd eventually add to the "Radio Free Insanity" opening theme. I couldn't have asked for a more recognizable voice in wrestling to speak the words: "Now, wait a minute. Did you say 'Radio Free Insanity' or 'Insanity Free Radio'? Which is it?"

I wasn't sure if he was kidding, so I told him he could call the show whatever he wanted. And then Jerry said, "I was going to try to give you an Insanity Free interview here today, but that doesn't happen much with me."

The surprises kept on coming. In what was the most amazing part of our entire discussion, Lawler seemed less-than-thrilled with the timing of his Hall of Fame induction.

"My luck, of all things," he said. "Most people realize I've been a lifelong Cleveland sports fan. Cleveland Browns and Cleveland Indians. It's just . . . you know, what's it? Murphy's Law? Worst thing that can happen will happen. The Cleveland Indians, my favorite baseball team, happen to be playing for the first time in the franchise history and probably the last time in the franchise history, they're playing the last exhibition game of the spring training season in my hometown of Memphis on the exact same night I'm being inducted into the Hall of Fame."

Jerry went on to say that he had already made plans to have some of his friends from the team come by to see his house. Then, he let out a big sigh and said, "Not anymore. I'm gonna be inducted into the Hall of Fame." It was like hearing a kid say, "Guess I don't get to go to Six Flags, because I have to go to the stupid dentist."

It threw me. From watching WWE television, all you ever hear inductees say is that it's one of the best things to ever happen to them. They put on WWE Hall of Fame shirts and tell stories about how Vince McMahon destroyed the people that helped them get started. You rarely hear them say that they're pissed off about the scheduling of their induction.

At first, I actually thought he was joking. (It goes back to that whole serious and funny at the same time thing.) I told Jerry to look at the bright side: at least he got to call games for the XFL. That didn't go over well. Lawler thought I was being serious, and said he'd enjoyed that experience. Go figure, what were the odds that he'd be one of the ten people who enjoyed the ill-fated football league.

But what I really liked about interviewing the King was that he was so easy to interact with. It probably has something to do with his years of color commentating, but he picked up on everything I said and had an immediate and interesting reply. And just like on television, he was willing to joke about himself to make the interview more entertaining. The best example of this came as I was making a point about how his television character had somehow become a good guy. A longtime villain, Lawler seemed to turn overnight, without the aid of a major angle.

"As a wrestler," I said, "when you usually go from a bad guy to a good guy, there's usually a big angle. Your friend turns on you. Your girlfriend suddenly becomes, you know, a prostitute, and hates you . . . but with you . . ."

Jerry laughed, "That's happened to me many times!"

It was his ability to joke about his own life that made Lawler such a pleasure to talk to. There was nothing deceptive about him. Everything good about Lawler was out in the open. And all of his faults were too. People don't love Lawler because of what he's done to win them over; they love him because he's a lovable guy.

Usually wrestlers currently employed by a big company are nothing if not highly diplomatic during interviews. It's rare that they'll really shoot. When asked about a rival promotion, they politely acknowledge them, claim superiority, and move on. When I asked Jerry the "TNA question," he answered as only the King can.

"Honestly, I do not get to see it. I think, in all its existence, I saw part of one show. . . . And I know a lot of people will say, 'Oh yeah . . .' But it really is true. I just don't . . . get the opportunity to watch it. I mean, you know . . . like whenever it's on, I'm usually doing something more important, like sorting my socks, checking my teeth for plaque, or renewing my subscription to *People*."

In typical Lawler form, he built up the first half of his answer in complete seriousness, then came out of nowhere with his punch line. Maybe it's my sense of humor, but when it comes to pure delivery, Lawler has everyone beat. He's a master.

The King has an uncanny knack for bringing a joke out of nowhere; he does it weekly on *Raw*, and he did it during his ClubWWI interview. When people ask me about the funniest thing I ever heard from a guest, I tell them about Lawler addressing his concern about overstaying his welcome during his Hall of Fame acceptance speech. It's the hardest I've ever laughed during any interview.

"What comes to mind in the past three or four Hall of Fame ceremonies . . . is how long-winded some of these guys are. I love Superstar Billy Graham. But it's kind of been a running joke . . . I don't know if you heard the Superstar's acceptance speech, but you know, he started talking out about the fact that . . . some young lady died in a car crash. He received one of her organs in a transplant. And without that, he probably wouldn't be alive today. . . . Then he went on from that to . . . his wrestling career . . . By the time Superstar Graham was through, I was starting to wish that young lady was a better driver."

I couldn't believe he said it. And I love that he did.

Another guest that didn't disappoint was Diamond Dallas Page. He was everything I had hoped, and then some. Even after being on air with him for 80 minutes, and for 40 minutes before the show started, DDP never lost a beat. He's the real deal — and I wasn't sure I'd be able to say that before I spoke to him.

DDP

Diamond Dallas *is* Positively Page. He's Mr. Yoga and inner strength. Whenever I would parody him in a *Raw* Insanity, I'd have him doing Pilates or drinking wheat juice. He's like Tony Robbins meets the Dalai Lama meets The Fonz meets Dog the Bounty Hunter.

At first, I wasn't sure how much of this was legit, or how much was a gimmick. Of course, it doesn't take much to be cynical about wrestlers. And although some have tried to work me, many are genuine. DDP was one of the most genuine. After the sheer amount of time we spoke, uninterrupted, if he was lying to me, he'd have to be Sidney Poitier.

Page also provided perhaps the strangest pre-interview moment, ever — it's even got Jerry Lawler's breakfast beat.

When I called Dallas, he asked me to give him a few minutes.

To this day, I'm still not 100% sure what was going on . . .

I heard something humming, loud, like a car vacuum. It went on for about a minute before Page spoke phone again.

Bzzzzz! . . .

"Hang on. I'm almost done . . ."

Bzzzzz! Bzzzzz! Bzzzzz!

He tried to explain what was going on, but I couldn't make it out over the buzzing.

In support of my car vacuum theory, I'd occasionally hear a clunking, like a penny being sucked through a hose. Every time I'd hear this, it was followed DDP exclaiming, *"Shit!"*

For at least five minutes, I sat there and listened to Diamond Dallas Page vacuum his car . . . I think.

Then the buzzing stopped.

"I'm back."

I never asked what he was doing, but if it wasn't a car vac I don't want to know.

The first time I ever saw Dallas Page was when he was in the AWA. DDP was the manager of Sensei Pat Tanaka and Paul Diamond, better known as the Diamond Exchange. He was the poster boy for 1980s New Jersey Cool.

Through the years, no one can dispute how hard he worked to improve himself. "Stone Cold" Steve Austin, who ripped through the wrestling world, retired at the age of 37. DDP didn't start his first big run *until* he was 37. If you don't respect that, I don't know what to say.

Page wasn't even a wrestler when he started out. I remember his transition during the early 1990s in WCW, and it wasn't exactly smooth sailing. Still thought of as just a manager, Dallas had many people to win over. Years later, when he felt jilted by the nWo, he finally got his moment. No one clawed his way up the wrestling ladder like DDP.

He not only became a wrestler, he became a great wrestler. The Diamond Cutter highlights of the late 1990s simply blew people away. The WWF may have had Stunners galore, but the Diamond Cutter ruled the WCW roost.

 Dallas Page understands the importance of hard work better than anyone, and now, through his public speaking, he wants to teach others the same thing. While many fans will write it off as a sales pitch, you only need to listen to Page speak to understand how much it means for him to spread the word about yoga. It's part of who he is; he really believes in it and it's served him well. Sure, he's trying to sell it to you too, he doesn't deny that; but above everything else, it's something he believes in.

I wasn't going to give Dallas an easy run though. Just because he was a hard worker and a multi-time WCW Champion, I was still going to ask some tough questions. Aside from finally asking Shockmaster Fred Ottman about his legendary fall through WCW scenery, this was the one thing I'd always been dying to investigate: David Arquette. Yo, DDP, what the . . . ?

For those who don't know, David Arquette is, um, an actor. He was in *Scream, Eight Legged Freaks*, and is married to one of the *Friends*. He also starred in *Ready to Rumble*. You know, the movie about World Championship Wrestling?

And yes. It *was* cheesy.

Want to know what's even cheesier?

I own it on DVD.

Yeah . . . shut up. It's okay, I guess. There have been worse films. I wouldn't chuck the DVD into my fireplace . . .

But I also wouldn't make the movie's 160-pound star the real WCW Champ.

That's just what WCW did, and yes, it was terrible. Every wrestling fan on the planet died a little bit inside. Abe Lincoln rolled over in his grave.

DDP knew what was coming as soon as I brought it up.

"You worked with David Arquette during that, uh, memorable . . . moment . . . in WCW history . . ."

He let out a huge, fake laugh.

"You know, all's I know is that K-Fed beat the World's Champ. Now, let's go back in time. Let's go back in time . . . I don't want to hear no more shit about David Arquette being World Champ!"

Yes, he was right. Kevin Federline, then-husband of Britney Spears, had just defeated WWE Champion John Cena on Monday Night *Raw*. But Dallas wasn't going to put up any walls. He knows that the Arquette angle didn't play out. His laugh alone showed that he had real perspective. Sometimes you ask a guest about something and you expect them to be in on the joke . . . and then you realize that they're not.

"Columbia, South Carolina, was coming up on one of our shows, and that's the same town I got paralyzed in. I said, 'Let's turn something out here. Let's make it better.' So me and Rick Steiner and Scotty got together and we just sort of turned it out to make it better. We thought . . . [They said,] 'What about your mom wheeling you out and doing something where she was part of the whole deal?' And when that happened, the crowd went crazy for it. So, of course, everything we threw out on TV, if it worked, we just rolled to the next week. So it just kept rolling and rolling and rolling and she got more popular and more popular. Everybody wants to see a mom hit somebody or slap somebody. . . . It worked. It made for good ratings and good TV. So that's how it all came about."

— Buff Bagwell

Buff Bagwell

See what I mean? Judy Bagwell, Buff Bagwell's mother . . . former WCW Tag Team Champion and trendsetter for divas everywhere. Just when it couldn't get worse, the company put her on a forklift as part of a match stipulation. Ironically, who do you think interfered in this debacle? Yup, you guessed it. David Arquette. The insanity comes full circle.

So, when DDP laughed, at least I knew we were on the same wavelength.

Page went on to talk about how David didn't even want to be champion, claiming he had too much respect for the belt. That was pretty shocking to hear. I mean, there was an "outsider," a Hollywood actor, expressing more respect for the WCW title than the people who were in charge of writing the shows. For an old WCW fan, that's mind-blowing.

It's something you rarely hear: too many people involved with the Monday Night Wars try to make their point, and too few have taken the time to reflect, to sit back and think or listen. When given the chance to speak, DDP cleared the air, refusing to pretend that his friend David was a smaller, modern-day version of Lou Thesz.

Actually, I learned how important this kind of self-awareness was before I ever dreamed of interviewing wrestlers. . . .

CHAPTER EIGHT

TELEMARKETER TO THE STARS

"You got two ears and one mouth. So listen and keep your damn mouth shut!"
— My Old and Grizzled Sales Manager, circa 2001

My job is half-interviewing and half-telemarketing. From generating wrestler's numbers to contacting them and then conducting the discussions, everything's done on the phone.

Because of this, I follow many of the principles I picked up when I was younger, working in business-to-business sales. Unlike telemarketers who call your house and harass you during dinner, B2B callers follow a set of rules designed to help them close a deal with savvy individuals. You know, it wasn't: "Oh, hello. . . . Is your mommy home? No? How old are you? Five? Okay. Can you read numbers yet? Good . . . Do you know where mommy keeps her Visa card?"

There are tons of rules governing successful business-to-business calling: don't leave messages unless you've called a million times; ask for names of those who might lead you in the right direction to get to the person you're really looking for; most importantly, keep your mouth shut when the prospective client has been asked to buy. It puts them in an awkward spot and increases the chance they'll agree.

That last lesson was the big one, and it applies to face-to-face sales as well. Go into any sales office anywhere in the world and you're sure to hear the now legendary tales: "I said, 'Stu — you wanna buy or not?' He didn't say anything. So I didn't say anything.

We sat there in silence for nine days — just staring at each other — before he ordered."

Exaggerated? Sure. But the way things really work? Definitely.

Something else I picked up during my years in sales was that you should always tell your subject that you only need a few minutes of their time. Then, from there, you talk as long as you have to, to get the job done. If they stop you and say you ran out of time, then you've done something wrong. The grizzled old guy I quoted at the start of this chapter used to tell us that when a client would say, "I only have two minutes," he'd take off his watch, place it on the table, and say, "Fine, you time me." Nine times out of ten, two minutes would turn into 20.

And that's what I do with these interviews. I tell every guest that I hope to interview them for about 20 minutes. Most discussions usually last about an hour. It's not rocket science. If an interviewee is talking in-depth about subjects they want to discuss — about themselves — they're not going to stop because of what the clock says.

The only thing I do differently when it comes to calling wrestlers? I take "No" for an answer. I really don't believe there's any point in harassing someone into an interview they don't want to do. It's no fun for them; it's no fun for me. And it's especially not fun for my listeners. However, there is one thing that has to happen to make me follow this principle.

They actually have to say, "No."

Simple, right? Not so fast. For some reason, people have a hard time saying that little word, especially in the image-driven world of sports entertainment. I can only speculate that they're worried about being slammed by an interviewer's personal vendetta if they turn him down.

In my case, that would never happen. Some fans would never be able to guess the names of wrestlers who've refused to be on my show. I don't let it affect how I talk about those men and women on air. To me, they're simply different people. Like I've said, again and again, if I've learned anything it's that the person I speak to and the person on TV aren't the same. The line, "I'm not a _____, but I play one on TV" has never been more appropriate.

I also don't let the fact that someone's been on the show affect my judgment of their in-ring work. I've had guests on one week and then come down on them in my commentary the next. I view the product separately; it really has nothing to do with the people who create it.

So, in other words, I'm cool with "No." Tell me you don't want to be on — that's fine. But when I do manage to get a wrestler on the line, it's rare that they don't end up doing an interview. And when I do get the occasional polite and straightforward rejection, it actually makes me respect the person more. In an industry where so many people have learned to blow others off by not returning calls or e-mails, it's refreshing when someone just says they don't want to be on and then tells me why.

Some of the most common explanations I've heard have been that the performer just wants to move on — to a new stage in their life or a new career — or that they just don't want to sound bitter about the industry. That's something you have to respect.

Of course, I've had a rude rejection. There haven't been many, but one does stand out. It came from a star who disappeared in 2004, never to resurface again.

Before calling this particular guy, I asked the person who gave me the number, "So, what's the deal? Why does he have heat with everyone?"

The answer was just a bit enigmatic . . .

"Talk to him for ten seconds — you'll know."

I called, and breaking one of my own rules, I left a message the first time out, then waited. After two days, I called again. This time the former wrestler picked up.

"This is James Guttman, I was just calling back . . ."

"If I was interested in doing an interview, I'd have called you back. I'm not, so I didn't!"

Click.

My contact was wrong: the conversation lasted less than ten seconds and I still understood why people didn't like him.

Some people are like that — no wonder he got banned from UPN.

At least he turned me down with a direct answer. Plenty have given me the run-around. I've had wrestlers schedule interviews and then simply disappear. To me, that's ridiculous. Why say, "Call me tomorrow at three," if you just don't want to talk? "No" is so much simpler.

"No."

See? There. Like that.

I'm not selling Amway. If you're not down with the idea of an interview, I'm not going to call you every night. However, if you do say you'll do it as long as I call back . . . I'm going to call back until I actually speak to you. In most cases, persistence pays off, and the modicum of professionalism actually makes guests, who might otherwise not be interested, warm to the idea of appearing on ClubWWI.

Case in point? Bobby "The Brain" Heenan.

Bobby "The Brain" Heenan

Heenan's was the first "uncut" interview I offered on ClubWWI, the day after the site opened, and I couldn't have picked a better person for the opening spot. The Brain is simply spectacular in everything he's ever done and he has a sense of humor that people who have worked with him say is on the level of the world's most legendary comedians. And that's not an exaggeration.

Heenan's discussion lasted nearly an hour and was a true pleasure. Any fan of '80s wrestling knows that "The Weasel" was leaps and bounds above most of his peers in terms of his skill with the mic. The banter he created with Gorilla Monsoon could make me laugh harder than most stand-up comics of the time, and when I finally got a chance to interview him in September 2006, I was thrilled.

But my journey toward that interview actually began almost a year earlier, in November of 2005. Then, with just a few editions of "Radio Free Insanity" in the can, I knew Heenan would be a major coup. I dialed the number I'd been given and waited patiently until a familiar voice picked up and answered rather abruptly.

"*Hello.*"

Bobby put emphasis on the "hell" in "hello," and it threw me off. At the same time, given my inexperience with reaching out to interview subjects, I guess I didn't expect him to answer directly. I'm not sure what I was expecting, to be honest. Would he have an assistant? Maybe a Rosatti sister? Jameson?

"Hi . . . Bobby? This is, uh, James Guttman. I'm from World Wrestling Insanity . . ."

"Insanity? World Wrestling Insanity?"

It would become a running theme for the next few years, happening whenever I'd call someone unfamiliar with the site. That's why I always breathe easy when my initial call doesn't begin this way — it means they know who we are. More and more, current stars seem to know, but legends who have been away from the business for a while usually require some . . . explanation.

"Yes . . . I was wondering if, well, we do . . . I mean, I do . . . interviews with people who are in the wrestling business . . . And I was hoping that . . ."

"I'm not going to — right now. Call me back in two months. I'm busy. Yeah. Busy. Can't talk. Goodbye."

Click.

Well, that sucked. I stood motionless for a second and thought about how I had just blown the chance to interview someone I'd always dreamed about speaking with. If I had to make a list of guests I was most interested in having on the show, Heenan would have easily made the top ten. And he'd just blown me off.

Except . . . except that he said the magic words, "two months." So, as I was taught during my time in sales, if you're given a time to call back — call back. No matter how far away the date might seem. No matter when they say — if you're still in business — circle the date on your calendar and then make the call. If someone says, "Call me in 2095," make sure your grandkids make the call for you.

Two months later, I called Bobby Heenan for the second time. It was now January 2006.

"*Hello.*"

"Hey, Bobby. This is James Guttman of World Wrestling Insanity."

"Hello . . ."

"Hi . . . I was just checking to see if you'd be interested in doing that interview with us. I've interviewed a number of different people in the business. Vince Russo, Spike Dud. . . ."

"Call me back in April. Goodbye."

Click.

Dammit.

But hey, wait, he said, "April."

So I waited for the snow to melt and the birds to start singing. April showers and all that nonsense. And then I dialed the Brain once more. He answered as usual: *"Hello."*

I gave my pitch, and this time he *remembered* my name. He told me that he was going to be at *WrestleMania,* and that he would be away for a while. But he also said he would be ready to do an interview at the end of the summer. He asked me to call back then. And so I did.

As many know, Bobby had been diagnosed with throat cancer and was taking medication as part of his treatment. When I initially called back in September, he asked if we could postpone the interview until the following week because he wasn't feeling up to it. Of course, I understood. And given the fact that we'd been going back and forth for a year of two-minute phone conversations, I figured a one-week push-off was as close as I'd come yet. I happily called back the following week.

What followed was one of the most enjoyable interviews I've ever done. Heenan was very appreciative of the fact that I pushed back the discussion in light of his medical issues. Maybe he'd expected me to complain or tell him that we needed to get it done right away, but I didn't want it to be like that. I never do. To me, it wasn't even a question of whether I could push it back. It was simply the right thing to do. And maybe because I had been accommodating, the Brain spoke with me for nearly an hour. Even with the difficulty he had talking, Bobby still spoke at length and was as witty as I remembered. It's one of the interviews I'm most proud of — the fact that Bobby Heenan, recovering from throat cancer, spoke to me on-air for so long is something I'll never forget.

Another example of how tenacity paid off in the long term is the interview I eventually secured with Sean Mooney. Sean was a WWF announcer for many of their formidable years. From 1988 to 1993, fans saw Mooney more than they saw Hulk Hogan. He hosted Event Center, WWF's "Live Events" Calendar, and was featured following each match on the program. Sean was friggin' everywhere. . . .

I first contacted Mooney shortly after the site opened in October 2005. I'd only done three shows, and to paraphrase rasslin' jargon, I was greener than broccoli vomit on a pool table. He told me to call back a few days later.

I did.

He didn't answer.

I was sad.

As the months rolled by, I revisited that Mooney number often. I tried him time and time again. After all, this guy was the "one that got away" from the wrestling industry. (It's a phrase that he himself used to describe how he's perceived.) In a business where almost no one gets out in one piece, Sean not only escaped, but he never looked back. There were no Sean Mooney TNA appearances or MySpace shoots. He was just out. Gone.

It took two and a half years for me to get Mooney on the phone again. I never mentioned my original approach from '05 — that was the past.

Once again, he agreed to do the shoot.

Once again, I called and he wasn't there.

This time I called back right away. I left messages. I tried almost every day. Again, all I needed was a "No" and I'd disappear . . . but until that word was spoken it would be me and Sean's voicemail — daily.

A few days later, when my caller ID finally said Sean Mooney, I was expecting to hear that "No."

"James? Sean Mooney. You've a very persistent man . . . I'll give you that."

He may not have realized how much that meant — I prided myself on the tenacity with which I'd gone after interviews for my listeners. Having the guy who co-hosted *Prime Time Wrestling* say those words made me feel like it really was the right way to do what I do. The 12-year-old boy in me was going nuts. (I mean that in the "inner child" sense. I don't eat children . . . that's how wrestling rumors get started.)

Sean and I spoke for a while and, quite naturally, we just eased into the interview. It was his first shoot interview ever — which in the grand scheme of wrestling history is pretty shocking. And it's not because he's never been asked. . . . Mooney had turned down invitations from tons of outlets, including WWE.com. Just as with Eric Bischoff, it was like I got to him at the right time, or said something that made him eager to speak out.

One of those things that made him speak may have been his desire to clear up rumors that he hated the wrestling business. In reality, the opposite was actually true. But understanding that anything can be spun, Mooney had simply opted to keep his opinions to himself so they wouldn't be misconstrued. The last thing he wanted was to be misquoted and come off like a WWE hater — he was anything but.

I assured him that wouldn't happen. To be completely honest, I find that the interviews people like best are with people who don't want to go postal on everyone in Titan Tower. Fans today are highly sensitive to bitterness and can tell in a minute how skewed your opinions are by personal vendettas. Those who still have a fondness for wrestling, and even the McMahons, make the best subjects for that reason: they can tell in-depth stories happily, without spending too much time trashing today's product. That's what people really want to hear: negative interviews may sell sometimes, but interesting interviews sell all the time. Because I try to keep things positive, Sean Mooney, the guy whose face was as much a part of my Saturday mornings as Zack Morris and *The Snorks*, agreed to give me his first in-depth wrestling shoot interview ever.

Over time, I've learned to improve my technique, but I really got a crash course in the art of the interview when the site first opened.

I was doing a lot of radio interviews myself at the time to promote my first book. From *Jim Bob and The Morning Chicken Show* to *Weiner and The Butt* to *Dropkick Billy's Wrestlerama Hour*, I did all the big ones. . . .

One thing that is just no fun is when you realize the person you're speaking with has done no research whatsoever. I'll never forget doing the interview where the host welcomed me to his show with, "So . . . what do you do?"

Because of this, I research the hell out of my interviews. As soon as I set my sights on someone for the show, I begin reading about them as much as I can. Guests more than appreciate it when they realize you know who they are, what they've done, and where they worked.

There's a big difference between saying, "You were trained by Ivan Koloff. What was he like?" and "Who trained you? Ivan Drago or some shit like that?"

Knowing a wrestler's history is a show of respect and, believe it or not, it actually comes in handy in the long run . . . I never could understand the point of memorizing stats and dates. Many hard-core wrestling fans can do it though, and it's both impressive and bizarre at the same time. Why would you ever need to know the main event and location of the 323rd episode of *Raw*? That just seems a little *too* involved. I mean, there's just so much stuff to remember.

And I know I've already mentioned this, but I want to make something else perfectly clear: I'm not here to argue with anyone for argument's sake. I've never been able to understand it. Some fans want you to be confrontational; they expect you to call people out. Potential guests are always a little worried about being made to look foolish on-air — that's just part of the territory with some wrestling fans. But I'm not looking to create a Howard Stern-like comedy spot.

That kind of thing would be stupid, and I'll tell you why: who really wants to engage in a conversation with someone asking nothing but embarrassing questions or trying to get a rise out of them? My goal is simply to be the reasoned voice of the average listener. If there's a good question to ask, even if it's difficult, I'm going to ask it. But I'll never attack someone just to make "good talk radio." I want the people I'm interviewing to be relaxed, comfortable enough to open up.

I'm on your side. . . . Tell me your story. . . . For this week, at least, the floor is yours.

At the end of the day, who the hell am I anyway? What gives me, or any other fan, the right to argue with the people who come on my show to discuss their career? Even in the case of my guest hosts, men and women I know best, that never happens. It doesn't matter how familiar I am with a guest, they're the ones who spent years working in the business. And I'm the one who spent years watching and enjoying them.

But this brings up the issue of correcting misconceptions or mistakes. My goal in doing these interviews isn't to prove I know the facts, or that a guest has got something wrong. That's something else I've been stuck by. There is no point in forcing it, and in the end, you run the risk of unintentionally shaping what your subject has to say.

Wrestling, as I've said, is a lot like any insular community. Rumors fly and go from ear to ear about every member of the roster. Remember high school? We had a shop teacher that some people said ran over his wife with a motorcycle. Did he? Who the hell knows? No one ever verified the story. Actually, a story circulated that someone asked him about it and he admitted that it indeed happened. But then no one could verify the story about whether or not it was verified! Now keep in mind . . . I went to that school and even I don't know the facts. Imagine how convoluted some of these stories are by the time they reach the ears of those who've never stepped foot into a wrestling locker room.

Rumors are usually pretty far from reality. Whether it's a genuine misunderstanding, misreporting, or evil intentions that muddy the waters, they're the kind of thing that can make my job very difficult at times.

Some wrestling fans treat everything they read as gospel, and that's clearly not always a good idea. In fact, forget wrestling, you just shouldn't take any news as gospel. If Katie Couric tells you that the moon has just fallen from the sky, you might want to look out your own window before you start planning for Armageddon. The bottom line is that wrestling news is no different than "real" news. Almost everything you hear comes, at best, second hand. Remember, you weren't backstage — how are you ever going to know for sure?

Don't just take my word for it. Ask former news anchor and appreciator of persistence, Sean Mooney, "I hated doing news. I hated being a news anchor because it was just not something I wanted to do. I mean, people ask me, 'What was the difference between wrestling and news?' And I say, 'Well . . . at least wrestling admits it's fake now. I mean, that's the truth. It was just like that. I stayed in that world for five years and couldn't wait to get out."

And here's the kicker — and this is something I didn't even begin to understand until after I did a good number of interviews — sometimes, even when something *is* true, there are always some people who know a *completely different* story.

What do I mean?

Well, in 2007, I interviewed Sid Vicious. Psycho Sid was every-thing I expected, and then some. I mean that in a good way. As a kid, I thought he was the type of guy who didn't play around. Don't mess with Sid — he'll eat you.

In our interview, he was positive and cordial — and terrifyingly straightforward. He gave the benefit of the doubt to Ric Flair, *after* Flair had slammed him on WWE's Horsemen DVD. He guessed that maybe someone had told Naitch that he didn't appreciate the Horsemen . . . and that may have skewed Flair's opinion. After all, according to Vicious, Ric had always been nice to his face.

> "This is the honest to God's truth, Ric Flair has been one of the nicest people to me — to my face. And he has to do that; otherwise I'd slap the fuck out of him."
> **— Sid Vicious**

I loved the guy — interviews like his are easy. Sid didn't need

Sid Vicious

any prodding. Occasionally, I'd sense him trying to reel back and soften his candor, but it never lasted long. He is who he is, and that's precisely why I wanted him on the show in the first place.

One thing about his interview people still ask me about are his thoughts on the Chris Benoit/Kevin Sullivan split in WCW. The fabled departure of Benoit and some friends from World Championship Wrestling occurred because Kevin Sullivan had been put in charge of the show. In an effort to mollify the group, which was threatening to quit, WCW gave Benoit a World Title win . . . over Sid Vicious.

Now, I've always thought I knew the full story. Apparently not, according to Sid.

"People who were in charge, like Kevin Nash and Kevin Sullivan, those people like that . . . they were doing a pretty good job of using, you know, what I figured was the talent they had there. When Vince Russo came in, he started using guys like Chris Benoit, Dean Malenko, Perry Saturn, Shane Douglas. Nothing against those guys, because they're all good. They work really hard, okay? And Vince Russo is a really nice guy with stuff like this, but he was letting them have a lot of input. . . . They were getting way too crazy with it, like trying to figure out who they were working with at TV, before they got there . . . get all their schemes taken care of and stuff like that, which to me is ridiculous. I'm the type of person that needs to know when I get there — not days before. But what they were trying to do, and everybody knows this, they were trying to start a union to remove Kevin Sullivan and bring back Vince Russo. [WCW executive vice president] Bill Busch and everyone . . . already knew what they were up to. Bill Busch came up to me personally. I think he had a trust in some of the things he could ask me.

So he told me about it. I was told that day, that morning, at the gym, that I was dropping the belt to Chris and I thought it was a little shocking. Nothing against Chris, but if you put the World Title on someone who means nothing, to make them mean something . . . So that does make sense? To a certain degree, because he's such a hard worker . . . but not a credible World Champion. To me, [he's] like a Rey Mysterio. Not just that he wasn't pushed enough — Rey and Chris have been pushed really hard for a long time, and if you don't see it, then you're not watching the TV everyone else is seeing. They're really not World Champions that can carry a territory, you know, and I'm pretty much sure they didn't expect them to. When they came to me with that finish, they didn't make a big deal about my leg being under the [bottom rope]. They just said to make sure it is and that's your out. That's how you got beat, but they already planned what they were going to do."

Okay . . . so, for most fans out there, Chris Benoit's WCW reign is seen as an olive branch from management, extended in an effort to keep Benoit and his buddies in the promotion. That's not how Sid saw it, though. Why? Because, according to Sid, Benoit didn't quit anything . . .

"They were going to let him win that title, and for whatever reason, I don't know if it was some contract reason, where they said, 'Now we're gonna fire him.' So they did. As soon as that match was over, they fired all those guys . . . fired them all. They had Kevin Nash put the title back on me the next night with the same finish, with a Crossface. So that's what happens in this business. You can be silly and do silly things and the repercussions can be really silly too."

Wow, that's utterly unlike what many consider, at this point, to be accepted history. When people ask why I didn't correct him, I explain the various factors in play.

First, as I've said, who the hell am I to correct Sid Vicious about backstage WCW politics? You know where I was when Benoit jumped ship? I was 21 — I hadn't started writing about wrestling yet. And while I might not be able to tell you exactly where I was, I can tell you one thing for certain: I wasn't booked on *Nitro.*

Secondly, let's pretend I'm completely right and, sure, Sid's completely wrong. . . . (JG Note: Please don't kill me, Sid.) If he believes that Benoit and his buddies were fired, then that's what he believes and I want to know that. It affected how he dealt with the situation and influences how he views the players. I wouldn't be doing a good job if I wanted his opinions to be anything other than completely real. Without knowing what's behind his thought process, you'll never fully understand a guest or the reason for his actions.

It's just another facet of things behind the scenes that has both surprised me and yet seemed so logical in hindsight. Everyone's actions are affected by what they believe to be true. In the case of Sid, he's operated believing that Chris Benoit and the Radicals were fired by WCW.

The tone of the interview and the fact that Sid referred to Benoit in the present tense should give you an indication of when it took place. We recorded on June 11, 2007, exactly two weeks before Chris Benoit would murder his wife and son in a moment that shook the entire wrestling business to its core.

CHAPTER NINE

BENOIT AND THE FALLOUT

On June 25, 2007, Chris Benoit, former WWE Champion and meat-and-potato hero to die-hard wrestling fans everywhere, murdered his wife, Nancy, and son, Daniel, before taking his own life.

It was a day, and an act so inconceivably heinous, that wrestlers and wrestling fans alike will never be able to forget.

For many, it was as if Superman had returned from work and murdered his family. Chris Benoit was the kind of star fans followed like a religion. Compared to others in his field, he was the quintessential professional. He'd honed his craft over two decades and worked hard to make his matches the best they could be each time he stepped in the ring. While some guys can claim they'd wrestle a good match with a broom, the Canadian Crippler could do it with a broken broom. Hell, he could pull it off with an imaginary broom — he really was that good.

Fans were both angry and confused. Were we to erase Chris Benoit — title reigns and all — from our memory and simply continue? He was all over wrestling's recent history, with both WCW and WWE. How do you revisit your favorite matches and watch the man who would eventually take the lives of his wife and son? Would wrestling ever be the same?

I'm still not sure. With the passage of time, as a fan, I am able to watch Benoit's matches now. I don't necessarily cheer for him or his opponent, there's no point. I watch them to see the skill on display, the caliber of wrestling. That's all.

The guy could wrestle better than almost anyone on the planet: my interviews and private discussions with others in the industry helped me to understand that. And to be honest, if I hadn't learned to separate the wrestler from the person many years ago, there'd be a hell of a lot of grapplers I would never watch. Chris Benoit the person died a demented and broken man; there will never be any viable explanation for what he did. Had he not committed suicide, he'd have been vilified by the masses during what would have surely been the circus of his trial. As a wrestler, however, his work was second to none. No matter what he did at the end of his real life, Benoit's in-ring performances are the standard other performers should strive toward. Forget boycotting Benoit videos. A young, aspiring wrestler who doesn't watch the work of Chris Benoit to improve his own skills is an idiot, plain and simple. I'm not saying you should wear a Rabid Wolverine T-shirt to Christmas dinner, but I am saying studying his performances as if he were a textbook would pay off.

As a webmaster and interviewer, the Benoit tragedy became very complex for me. Like I've said, it was tough enough for fans. Dealing with people in the industry, Benoit's friends and coworkers and peers, however, was even harder.

Many of the people I speak to on a daily basis knew the Benoits personally. They would never be able to say, "I only knew the TV Chris." After all, they *did* know the real-life Benoit. Many of them truly liked the man. But they also had no clue what the hell had happened.

We all deal with death. When an older relative or friend passes away, you naturally miss them. The grief is difficult, but you eventually come to terms with their death.

When a younger friend dies, we search for meaning, a reason. You miss them. The grief is difficult, and you struggle to understand why someone so young had to die.

When a friend commits suicide we search for reasons, answers. The grief is difficult, and you struggle with their absence because, ultimately, they took themselves from your life.

But what are you supposed to feel or do when a friend commits suicide after murdering his family? How do you reconcile all the conflicting emotions? Is it okay to miss him? Is it okay to not miss him? How do you deal with the guilt when you feel for him at all? Does this change everything you ever knew about him? If he played a large role in your life, does any of that change? Do you have to change?

It's almost impossible to imagine. The stories I heard privately that week were tough to listen to. I spoke to men that wage wars on television, who power-bomb one another through tables every week, too distraught to put their thoughts into intelligible words. It was sadder than you could imagine and very difficult to describe to this day.

Around the time of the tragedy, I interviewed Les Thatcher. Les had worked with both Benoit and his wife, Nancy. He told stories about knowing them both early on and revealed his feelings for them. Guys like Orlando Jordan, Steve Blackman, Bull Buchanan, and D-Lo Brown also spoke about the situation on ClubWWI. The whole thing was a kind of blur, though; no one really knew what to say, or how to say anything that hadn't been said already. You found yourself repeating the same things over and over again. And it was all you *could* do.

"I'm not sure how he could do this."

"If you lined up 100 guys and asked me to pick out the one capable of this, Chris would be the last I'd pick."

"I'm not condoning what he did . . ."

After a while, everything sounded the same. Given how goofy the on-air wrestling product sometimes is, transitioning to and from such a serious subject was damn near impossible. From ultra-silly to ultra-serious in one night — the whole world flipped upside down.

The situation couldn't have occurred at a stranger time.

Nancy Benoit had been in the business forever. Long before she met Benoit, she was married to Kevin Sullivan. The former WCW taskmaster was one of wrestling's most respected minds and had handled booking duties for many different companies. Alongside then-wife Nancy (a.k.a. Woman or Fallen Angel), Kevin played the demonic heel wherever he went.

When he and Nancy split, it was a public spectacle. Playing out in wrestling's fantasy TV world at the time, on WCW *Nitro*, Nancy was falling for Chris Benoit. Soon, as fans learned, what was a storyline spilled out into the real world.

The Benoits' marriage eventually became wrestling's version of Brad and Angelina: fans had witnessed a romance blossom in real life through the scripted world of WCW.

This led to a variety of problems. As I said, Sullivan was known for being the man booking WCW's programs. In essence, he figured out who'd win matches or become a champion. In 2000, the buck stopped with the Prince of Darkness.

Needless to say, Benoit wasn't happy about the situation. Worried about what his WCW future would hold, Chris left the company, alongside Eddie Guerrero, Dean Malenko, and Perry Saturn, just one day after winning the World Title from Sid Vicious — a move that Sullivan scripted in a show of good faith.

Kevin Sullivan with "Woman"

Almost a decade later, in April 2007, Kevin Sullivan was enjoying semi-retirement, while Chris Benoit was feuding heavily with WWE up-and-comer Montel Vontavious Porter. Times had changed, but I still wanted to hear the story behind it all. That's when I called Kevin for the first time.

When my call was answered, I knew, immediately, that it had to be Sullivan. Kevin is really famous for three things:

1. He's short but stocky. In a business where most men under 5'8" weigh 100 pounds and have to defy gravity to survive, Kevin was jacked.

2. His finishing move involved him jumping off the top rope and landing on an opponent's stomach with both feet. It looks crazy, and as a young fan, that move was the one thing that kept doubts about whether or not wrestling was "real" lingering in my mind.

3. He has a crazy thick Massachusetts accent. Wicked thick.

When he said hello, his voice sounded exactly as I remembered from years of promos — he was the real deal. He was also leaving for vacation when I called. Sullivan was very nice, though, and gave me his number to call back in May. That's what I did.

Our interview took place on May 7th, just one month before Chris Benoit would murder Nancy and Daniel. In hindsight, the timing was chilling. In preparation for the interview, I had immersed myself in research about Sullivan's relationship with Benoit. Little did I know how topical all of this would soon become.

I went into the interview expecting Sullivan to be close-lipped about Benoit. After all, that situation had to be embarrassing. Your wife runs off with another wrestler and then that wrestler threatens a mass exodus unless you're fired? That's got to be rough, right? But what choice did Benoit really have? After all, Kevin was going to bury him . . .

Amazingly, Sullivan, even after all he went through, was both frank and reasonable.

> "They were talent. I just made [Benoit] World Heavyweight Champion. I look at it as business. All of them were talented. I was gonna make Malenko and Saturn the tag team champions and Eddie was going to be U.S. Champion. Whatever the situation was, personally, when I was doing business, I looked at it business-wise. I lost them; I lost Jeter; I lost Giambi; I lost Rodriguez; I lost Posada. I left a big hole in the lineup. I wasn't stupid enough to let my own personal problems get in the way."

So, right, like I said, he was going to bur — wait, what? Really? That doesn't sound like a burial to me. And how many people have stopped to consider what that World Title change really entailed?

> "Do you know how hard it was to tell Sid Vicious that he's tapping out? Sid didn't want to do it, and I said I would appreciate it if you did. . . . He was gentleman enough to do it."

Another interesting point: when Sid appeared for his interview, if anything was perfectly clear, it was that he was focused on his character. If he didn't think something was right for him, he wasn't going to do it. And if you were going to ask him to do something difficult, you had better be respectful about it. . . . Evidently, Sullivan was.

As Kevin explained the situation, it became clear that he wasn't really looking to screw anyone over. If nothing else, it seemed like he had no problem separating business from the personal. As someone who had booked shows for decades, it was nothing he hadn't dealt with before. I remember finishing our discussion and coming away with a new sense of Chris Benoit's paranoia. While working with Kevin was never going to be fun or easy, there was no reason they couldn't be productive . . . and there was certainly no valid reason for all the drama.

Little did I know that Benoit's paranoia would soon become the subject of national *Geraldo-* and *Nancy Grace*–like television broadcasts. The stories that came out day after day, about Benoit's mental state, seemed to make sense given my recent interview. Think about it. How many wrestlers have left a company the day after winning the World Title because they're concerned about what the boss might do to their career?

That's perhaps the main reason I've never been able to blame anyone or anything for the Benoit tragedy except for Chris Benoit himself. Sure, the stress of his position and career path may have made his mental issues worse, but it clearly seems like he was already demonstrating paranoid tendencies years earlier. And I still can't help but think that even 1,000 other guys in Benoit's exact physical and mental condition would never have acted as he did . . . not even close. Vince McMahon and WWE didn't commit murder. Chris Benoit did.

It angered me when people began blaming the tragedy on steroids and other drugs. Saying illegal or un-prescribed substances were to blame is like handing Benoit a "Get Out of Responsibility Free" card. You can't blame drugs for this any more than you can blame an energy drink for making a streetracer slam into a building. But some people went even further, blaming Vince McMahon for allowing Chris Benoit to take the drugs that they say caused him to murder his wife and son. So now the man who committed the actual crime is at least two steps away from responsibility. First you blame Vince and wrestling, then the drugs, then Benoit? It's like the song about the woman who swallowed the spider to catch the fly.

For a while, in the media, it was loony tunes. People were blaming Benoit's pills. They were blaming his boss. It made no sense. How could CNN and Fox News devote so much programming to this? When a mailman shoots up the office, do we crucify the Postmaster General on Court TV?

Ironically, the best explanation for it all came from former wrestler Marc "Johnny B. Badd" Mero on an episode of *Nancy Grace:* "We have a platform to make a difference here . . ."

Jimmy Hart interviews Johnny B. Badd

Yeah, right. A platform. But you're building a platform on the bodies of an innocent woman and child. Way to go, Mero.

And here's why I really took exception to it all: if Marc wanted to really make a difference, then this could have been the perfect opportunity to present a plan of action. However, he and others like him did little more than work to tie the tragedy to all the other names on a "list" of wrestling's lost performers. Mero's list featured the names of wrestlers who had passed away in the last 20 years. It overflowed with wrestlers who died at an early age. And yes, it was a startling compilation, enough to shock fan and non-fan alike.

Curt Hennig . . . Rick Rude . . . Eddie Guerrero . . . Road Warrior Hawk . . .

All great stars who admittedly fought addiction and ended up losing their lives way too early.

Owen Hart . . .

Okay, that was a stunt gone tragically wrong, but it happened at a PPV, so technically it could count.

Junkyard Dog . . .

Um . . . he was in a car accident. He wasn't even driving to a show. He was driving to his daughter's graduation.

Earthquake . . .

Come on, he had cancer!

Was Johnny B. smoking crack?

It's part of the problem with pundits like Mero. As a former wrestler, he seems to subscribe to the theory that you need to pad any argument, no matter how convincing it already is. It's the same mentality that makes Hulk Hogan say Andre the Giant was nine feet tall when he slammed him; it's why Kurt Angle says that TNA does 15.5 ratings. The business is a work . . . and so some guys parlay that into their interview time too.

In Mero's case, he could have presented the list of those whose deaths could be clearly linked to drug abuse and people still would have taken notice. That list would still be far too long. Instead, he confused the issue by including guys like Yokozuna, whose death had more to due with obesity than any other factor.

Right off the bat, he's given people something to pick apart, already given his opponents good points to fight him on. People like Hennig and Guerrero get lost in the shuffle when you're busy defending your decision to include Brian "Mark Curtis" Hildebrand, another cancer victim.

On top of that, Mero further played this as if it were a wrestling angle by trying to insinuate himself into a situation that he had little or nothing to do with so he could get attention. In wrestling, it happens all the time. Floyd "Money" Mayweather is hot . . . so WWE brings him in for *WrestleMania* to get some attention. Donald Trump attacks Rosie O'Donnell, so WWE stages a fight between two look-a-likes. You follow the hype, you follow the money . . .

And so Johnny B. Badd busts his glittery butt to tie his list to the tragic deaths of Nancy and Daniel Benoit. It did nothing more than muddy the waters of a situation that most people could in no way fully comprehend. He did the wrestling business a disservice. He did the memories of Daniel and Nancy Benoit a disservice. And, in the most ironic twist, he did his own agenda a disservice.

By trying to attach his message to a tragedy it had nothing to do with and fluffing his list with unjustifiable entries, Mero may have steered more people away from his side than he would have if he just found his own forum. Had he not included guys like Owen and JYD in his argument, he would have been more convincing. Had he not tried to jump on the get-Benoit bandwagon, his "list" flopping in the breeze, he would have been more convincing. In the end, it seemed like a desperate plea for attention. Now, I'm sure there're plenty of guys who would love to see the wrestling business change, but I'm also pretty sure that many of them are wishing that Marc would get off their side. . . .

The Benoit situation also taught me an unexpected lesson about the effect of irresponsible mainstream journalism. (Note: my interview with Sean Mooney was still a year away.) As someone who dedicates so much time to giving wrestlers and wrestling a place to communicate with fans, it made me angrier than almost anything I'd ever experienced. You see, I've always thought of contemporary TV news as entertainment — first and foremost. Let's not kid ourselves. The teasers you see for today's news broadcasts would be considered parodic 20 years ago. Today's society is used to teasers that scream, "Is Angelina Jolie pregnant? News at 10! " Back in the proverbial day, it wasn't so blatantly . . . sensational, for lack of a worse term.

Nancy Grace has offered me up more entertainment than most. I was a big fan of *Court TV* when she was one of their talking heads. Grace has always cracked me up, with her steadfast self-assuredness — it's unwavering, even when she doesn't know what she's talking about or when she's making predictions based on gut-feelings. She speaks as if she's reading from an encyclopedia.

I still think of this one today. My wedding took place just a week before Jennifer Wilbanks disappeared before her wedding day. She vanished into thin air, and the whole world waited and prayed. Today, most know Wilbanks as the "Runaway Bride." It wasn't like that at the time, though. Back then she was the "Probably Dead Bride."

And that's precisely what Nancy believed too. I'll never forget watching CNN during my honeymoon and listening to her pontificate. One guest theorized that it was probably cold feet. Amazing Grace was having none of it: "Let me tell you one thing. Let me say just one thing. This . . . is not . . . cold feet."

And then she stared directly into the camera in a way that made you expect a mystery movie piano riff to follow: "Dum-dum-*dum!*"

Of course, a few days later the world learned that Wilbanks's feet *were* cold in the not-dead kind of way. We also learned that Nancy Grace talks without thinking.

Predicting a case's outcome is one thing; dealing with set-in-stone facts is another. I wanted to believe that the people responsible for presenting the news at least did some research about the history and the individuals they were reporting on. When the Chris Benoit tragedy came along, however, I learned the sad reality.

The folks putting the coverage together desperately wanted the story they *wanted to tell* to stick. They wanted it to be a story on steroids or deaths in wrestling. No one really wanted to cover the tragic murder of Nancy and Daniel, and that's another tragedy. With everyone debating whether Marc Mero's "list" was accurate or whether WWE drug tests were "real," no one took the time to mention that Nancy Benoit was a worker in the industry; both she and her young son were swept under the rug. Worse, a cavalcade of former stars marched onto TV, placed their soapbox on that rug, and blamed everything on wrestling.

I mean, let's get serious here. Debra Marshall-McMichael-Austin showed up on Fox News and held professional wrestling accountable for the fact that her ex-husband, Stone Cold Steve Austin, allegedly abused her. It was as she attempted to tie her ex's industry into why he was the way he was behind closed doors, that the true insanity of it all hit me. No, I'm not talking about the fact that Deb was saying this, I'm actually referring to the fact that a news anchor salivated over her every word without saying, "Are you effin' kidding me, lady?"

How ludicrous was this? Blame wrestling for steroid use? Fine, I can understand that, to a point. Pill popping? Sure. Drinking? Okay

. . . but we're stretching it. But domestic violence? Come on. Go to a battered women's shelter and take a poll. What tops the list of the careers of the men who drove the women there? Wrestlers?

I don't think so.

The most infuriating thing about the former purveyor of "Puppies" was that she said she could relate to what Nancy went through. Talk about crazy. Nancy had just been murdered. Debra was on national TV, wearing the same push-up bra she wore in the WWE.

Bill DeMott, better known to fans as Hugh Morrus, appeared on Fox with Debra. And DeMott, a respected trainer and performer, was having none of it. When I interviewed him for ClubWWI.com a few weeks later, he explained why people like her annoyed him. He sums it all up perfectly.

> "Before I was a professional wrestler, no one knew who I was. They gave me an opportunity, and for lack of a better term, made me famous, made me a lot of money at times, and gave me a lot of opportunities I never would have had in Paramus, New Jersey. Here came a girl I'd known for years — both from WCW and WWE. And I guess everything is fine with the world when you're getting paid and famous and in the limelight. But the minute you're not . . . the world really wasn't that great. Well, that kinda makes you a knucklehead. It makes you a knucklehead to sue someone who makes you famous just because you don't do it anymore. It makes you a knucklehead to blame a business that, while you were in it, you could put up with it. While you're making six figures, you can put up with the crap you went through and the people who did it to you and how bad everything was in your world. But to jump on a bandwagon during a tragedy . . . It pissed me off on a whole bunch of different levels. There's no need for it. Vince [McMahon] is a big boy; he can defend himself. I was defending wrestling."

I couldn't agree more. Blind loyalty to wrestling is ridiculous. You don't just sit back and allow the business to hurt people — but when someone blames it for woes it's not responsible for, people like Bill need to defend it. The mainstream media sure as hell won't.

Fancy Nancy and her not-cold feet ain't gonna either.

One more thing that affected me at the time relates back to Kevin Sullivan. And it, too, was truly awful.

A few weeks prior to the Benoit tragedy, Sensation Sherri passed away. Sherri Russell was a great person. She was supposed to be a part of my first book, but we didn't get her Q and A done in time. Sherri was someone I'd always planned to shoot with too, but the timing just never worked out. When I heard she'd died, people in the industry who were close to her told me many stories. She had always been very nice to me, but listening to those who knew her best, it became apparent that she really moved people.

Mainstream media outlets, which up until that time were unconcerned about the rate at which contemporary wrestlers pass away, looked for insane links to tie everything together. Sherri died just weeks before Nancy? There's a story there, right?

That was the thinking that must have gone into the coverage the day that someone told me to check out the Fox News website. I still can't believe what I read.

The headline told readers that they were looking into a shocking connection: Kevin Sullivan, the ex-husband of Nancy Dais-Benoit, had once been . . . Sensational Sherri's booker!

The irony in Sherri's stage name featuring the word "sensational" should not be lost in all this.

Sure, Kevin was her booker. He was also the booker for Sid Vicious, Perry Saturn, Three Count, Van Hammer, and about 1000 other people. Brian Pillman's infamous "I respect you, Bookerman" line was directed at Sullivan, for crying out loud. He was the booker, at one time or another, for many of the world's most influential wrestling promotions.

D-Lo Brown once told me that everyone in wrestling is connected: you can throw a rock at a crowd and hit five people you've worked with. It's hard for some to grasp, but with wrestlers moving from territory to territory, especially in Sherri's day, almost everyone shared ties.

But, of course, the mainstream media has no idea what a "booker" is. And they never bothered to find out. They assume it's an agent or manager — "He must book her dates." It would have taken five minutes of research — less time than it took to make the stupid image that illustrated the article — to realize that this non-story should have been killed way before it ever ran.

But no, there it was. Kevin Sullivan's name had been brought into the tragedy. I was sick to my stomach when I read it.

The bottom line here is that Kevin Sullivan was Nancy's ex-husband. She ran off with Chris and then, later, Benoit and the Radicalz left WCW. Kevin had done nothing wrong — except lose his wife and then get punished, professionally, for it. He'd been hammered over and over again for it and still tried to maintain some professionalism, and dignity, in the process.

Seeing Kevin dragged into everything on the basis of twisted facts and the public's ignorance of wrestling terminology bothered the hell out of me. And no matter how you feel about him, he certainly doesn't deserve to be splashed across the Fox News web page. Sullivan deserves respect — without him, wrestling simply wouldn't be what it is today.

Nancy Grace and Fox didn't have the market cornered on insanity, though. Hulk Hogan, who's great for a crazy sound bite now and then, offered his own. As many know, Kevin Sullivan played a Prince of Darkness gimmick. And yes, then-wife Nancy played his evil sidekick, Fallen Angel. But everyone knows they were characters they played on TV, right? Everyone?

Okay, everyone except Hulk Hogan.

How do I know? Because he had this to say to *Us Magazine:* "She was into devil-worship stuff. It was part of her [wrestling] character, but [she was] somebody who gets so close to their character, someone who gets into their character too much. Sometimes these people believe their own publicity. . . ."

This was eight days after the murders. Great job, brother.

Remember, this is the same guy who claimed that his son Nick had been misrepresented, his character skewed, shaped, and embellished by the reality TV show *Hogan Knows Best,* as he was trying to convince a judge to spare the young man prior to sentencing him for severely injuring a friend in a car accident. The unfairness of the camera and public perception affects only the Bolleas, I guess.

It's comments like this that made me desperate to have Hulk Hogan on my show. It's such out-of-left-field insanity that I had to hear him say this kind of thing myself. After all, he's the most successful crossover wrestling celebrity in the United States. Well, actually, no . . . he's the second most successful.

What? Oh, right. The Rock's second . . . So, fine, Hogan's slipped to #3 . . . Hey Hulkamaniacs, don't get mad at me — *I'm just telling it like it is.*

CHAPTER TEN

SAY IT LIKE IT IS, MAN

If you had asked me, when I first brought my site online, to name the wrestling celebrity I least expected to one day interview, I'd have picked former Minnesota Governor Jesse Ventura — hands down. In my mind, I had a better shot at interviewing Hulk Hogan ten times before I ever got to speak to "The Body."

Jesse "The Body" Ventura

Few people know that I was a political junkie growing up. In high school, I was the captain of my debate team, and even came back to serve as the team's coach after graduating. Politics had always been a passion, and in elementary school, teachers used to jokingly refer to me as Alex P. Keaton because I had a love for the political arena unlike the other kids in my class.

Yeah, I was a freak.

As I got older, my love for politics changed. Maybe it's a finely tuned bullshit detector that's to blame. I have a hard time glazing over and blindly listening to manipulated conversations. Sure, guests try to spin things on "Radio Free Insanity" all the time, and yes, I let them — but not because I don't realize what they're doing. I do it because it's their time to tell *their* story, whatever that story may be. Still, there have been times when I've mentioned to guests how obvious it was after the interview was over.

I still follow politics pretty closely though. Some people find it funny that I often have one of the "news channels" playing in the background when going about my day-to-day wrestling work. Sadly, that only serves to deepen my disenchantment. Try it yourself. Watch nothing but MSNBC or Fox for a week and experience their *Twilight Zone* version of the world for yourself.

You'll hear a politician make a speech on Monday. It's fine, and no one questions anything. Then, on Tuesday, his opponent will pick apart one particular sentence and explain it really meant something else. Next, the reporters, who had nothing to say about it on Monday, will suddenly jump to attention and spend hours debating what he or she *"really* meant."

Almost certainly it'll make you want to scream, "Weren't you people paying attention yesterday? We all heard the speech! You know what it meant! It's obvious!"

Then, after hours of yelling and via-satellite linkup debating, you get the real point. They *were* watching yesterday. Unfortunately, 24-hour news channels have airtime to fill today and tomorrow and the next day. By Friday, they're typically onto something else — there's always something new to misquote, another issue to purposely misunderstand.

The reason I first fell in love with my country's political system was that it offered people a chance to speak out. It was drilled into our heads as children. We were told that in the United States, we had the right to stand up and question. We, the people, could speak our mind without fear of persecution.

But that's almost impossible when you're too busy making sure you do not use an ambiguous word or phrase. There is no meaningful debate when questions not only yield no answers, but actually inspire the confusion of a barrage of talking heads picking apart the wording of the question itself.

In many ways, politics has become like professional wrestling.

No, not *fake* — although, wait, you actually have a point . . .

I mean, *scripted.* You know, like wrestling's promos and commentary. In WWE, we're routinely told that contracted stars are "shooting" straight from the heart. It's something I picked apart about Rob Van Dam's speech at the first One Night Stand. Fans applauded his "shockingly honest" speech about being held down. To me, and my trusty bullshit detector, it seemed like, well, Rob Van Blah-Blah-Blah.

The reason? Even when you try to present something like Van Dam's rant as "real," when it's scripted it will always necessarily betray elements of fiction. Their rhetoric goes over the top, like Van Dam explaining how all he ever wanted to do was succeed in this "great company" . . . you know, as opposed to, "Fuck this. Fuck you. Fuckedy-fuck-fuck — I'm out!"

Politics is like that too — big time. Politicians portrayed as straight-shooting try to come across as anti-Washington, but end up giving speeches right out of the bureaucratic playbook. It's enough to make you wonder if anyone will ever tell it like it is.

There's only one man I ever saw truly shoot during a wrestling broadcast. Of course, it happened when I was a kid. Nowadays, commentators are so over-prepared with scripts, prerecorded sound bites, and a producer yapping in their headset that even a random cough seems preplanned. In 1986, though, something actually occurred that, for me, lifted the veil from the business and showed that some things weren't as logical as the World Wrestling Federation would like you to believe.

Ironically, it all goes back to Hulk Hogan. The Hulkster was the WWF's King of Kings and he held the title with an iron grip. Everything he did was oh-so-good and everything the villains did was oh-so-bad. When King Kong Bundy would use a chokehold, Vince McMahon would scream from the broadcast table for a DQ. When Hogan would choke Bundy with his bandana for ten minutes straight, McMahon would laugh and scream, "Look at Hogan go!" That, my friends, was the way of the world, and all was good. (After all, you buy into the reality of the show you're watching.) If, in McMahonland, Hogan's cheating was justifiable, so be it.

What do you want? I was eight.

The first time I truly understood what this meant, I was watching an episode of *World Wrestling Federation Television*. That's right. The first time I truly questioned booking and the writing of the shows wasn't from a dirt sheet. And it wasn't because of the internet. Hell, the World Wide Web wasn't even a homunculus twisting around in Al Gore's brain back then . . . Hulk Hogan was wrestling Adorable Adrian Adonis. It was the blond-haired, blue-eyed babyface hero against the cross-dressing villain. You don't get much more clear-cut than that — and if you thought King Kong Bundy was held to a double standard, you ain't seen nothing yet.

In the mid-'80s WWF, a man in a dress was *always* wrong. No matter what.

During the match with Adonis, Hulk found himself blinded. It was an old gag, unable to see, Hogan flailed around, reaching out. He attacked turnbuckles, thin air, anything in his path. Unfortunately, during this blind spell, Hogan became locked in a sleeper hold. Then he did something he always did in this situation. He grabbed the referee by the shirt and started to whip him around. Vince McMahon and Jesse Ventura, the color commentators, watched from ringside.

Now, if Adonis had done this, McMahon would have pulled out a glock and shot him from ringside. After all, in the '80s, putting your hands on a referee was grounds for an immediate disqualification and post-match execution. Not for Hogan though. The rules were different for the Hulkster.

"He's blind! He's blind, Jesse! Look!"

Hulk continued thrashing the hapless ref.

And that's when Jesse finally voiced his opinion.

"Give me a break, McMahon!"

My immediate instinct, of course, was to boo Ventura. How dare he mock the blindness of our champion? McMahon reminded him once again that the Hulkster was tossing the official to and fro by his shirt because his vision was impaired.

Take that, Jess! How dare you? How dare you, sir?

"Oh yeah, McMahon? Let me ask you this. At what point in this match was Adonis wearing a shirt?"

Ha! Some comeback! Ha ha! "At what point in the match was Adonis wearing a . . ."

Hey, at what point *was* Adonis wearing a shirt?

Everything seemed to stop at that moment — my pre-teen mind froze. There it was. For the first time ever, a WWF heel commentator had made a strong point — one that you couldn't really refute — and proved that the Hulkster (gasp) was *cheating.* To be blunt — my world was turned upside down.

I mean, sure, Bobby Heenan was always great, funny as anything, but he never presented "real" points to discredit the good guys. He'd call Blackjack Mulligan a cheater, and when Gorilla Monsoon asked why, he'd say it was because he never washed his wrestling gear, that sort of stuff.

But Jesse Ventura was different. He was funny too, but the man who claimed to "tell it like it is," really did.

Man, imagine if this guy ran for office some day . . .

Fantasy became reality in 1990. Back then, the only non-underground or dirt sheet way to get wrestling news was from *Pro Wrestling Illustrated.* And it was there that I read the Body had just won the race to mayor in Brooklyn Park, Minnesota. Good for him, I thought. Still, it was hard to fathom that the evil Jesse Ventura actually ran a whole town.

If I thought that was insane, nothing prepared me for what would happen just eight years later. That's when the man who wore feather boas and bizarrely shaped sunglasses became the governor of Minnesota. Yeah, the state. The whole thing.

Talk about feeling like you'd woke up in the Land of Make Believe. I kept waiting for King Friday to show up on the carousel, declaring cooperation fun. It just made no sense. Political pundits couldn't believe it; wrestling fans couldn't believe it. I, at the wise old age of 21, couldn't believe it. It took a few days before I realized that I wasn't drunk.

Here was someone who had spent years, speaking straight mind you, in the wrestling business — an industry of "kayfabe" and endless "works." Now he was one of the most powerful political figures in the country? (You don't get much more worked than that.) I have to admit that I was a bit saddened to think that Ventura would become another talking head with manufactured "straight talk."

My BS meter was locked and loaded, waiting for the first onslaught of the Body's phony-baloney political "shooting."

At first, there were some superficial things that could have gone either way for Governor Ventura. For example, at times, the feather boa was still around his neck. It was hard to tell if it was a fashion statement, a worked attempt to seem true to himself, or something else. But in politics, words can be stronger than actions. . . .

And were they ever.

For the next few years, the Body made a point of speaking out in a way that would have been political suicide for anyone else. In fact, he gave an interview to *Playboy* less than a year after his victory that was enough to kill off 20 politicians. He spoke candidly about prostitution, legalizing marijuana, and other hot button issues. He also said, "Organized religion is a sham and a crutch for weak-minded people who need strength in numbers."

Yeah, he said that. The only spin to that statement is the one

The Governor backstage at WrestleMania *with Jimmy Hart*

where it spins through the air like a martial arts throwing star and stabs you in the face.

Now, I'm not saying that I agree with everything that Jesse Ventura says. But that's not really even the point. I didn't look up to him because we shared the same views. I looked up to him because we shared the same philosophy. No spin. No backtracking. No bullshit.

Jesse reminded me why I loved politics and affirmed that the things told to me by elementary school teachers were possible. Our responsibility as citizens is to speak out against what we don't agree with. Question authority. Debate freely. Do so without worry or prejudice.

When we fail to do that, we merely encourage frustration, apathy, and even violence. Those who have opposing views should feel allowed to express them without fear of persecution. When that fear exists, those with differing views can only express them with anger. The freedom to speak openly is what creates a society that functions for everyone. We need to be able to say, "I don't like organized religion," without someone threatening you or your family.

When you disagree with someone, tell them why. Explain your position. If you're truly resolute in your beliefs, you should be able to express them in a way that others can understand without any sort of aggressive behavior. It's the foundation of civilized society. It's something that had, in my eyes, been slowly disappearing from the world of American politics.

And that's why, in 2008, I was excited to read that Governor Ventura would be releasing a new book. *Don't Start the Revolution Without Me* promised the same straight talk we were all used to. To say it delivered would be a drastic understatement.

Jesse gave new meaning to the word "shoot." In a country where you're labeled un-American for questioning the policies of the U.S. following September 11th, Ventura took things a step further . . . questioning the September 11th attack itself. He referenced the Gulf of Tonkin, an admittedly manufactured event that brought the nation into Vietnam and compared it to the way the 9/11 attacks led us to Iraq.

It was the same thing that Rosie O'Donnell was raked over the coals for on *The View*. The difference was that Rosie didn't know enough about the history to back up her statement — Jesse wrote a few hundred pages about it. Also, Ventura is a former Navy Seal as well as a former governor — O'Donnell made a movie with Madonna and used to host VH1's *Stand-Up Spotlight*.

Rosie actually did her position a disservice. She was clearly unprepared to make an argument and instead made her point by screaming it out in a "gotcha" sort of way. That in no way represents my philosophy of how people need to speak out. It's just more of the same rhetoric we've heard far too often: if you yell loudly, people have to listen.

Jesse, however, was able to get his message out and at the same time encourage others to refute him in serious media forums. Sure, his 9/11 conspiracy theories are nothing new. Alex Jones, all sweaty and intense, has been yelling about it from behind a desk for years. David Icke has even gone so far as to claim that the Bush family is actually lizards and that they eat people. (I'm not kidding, that's his position.) Ventura's a national figure with a pro-U.S.A. resume that rivals anyone's. Not only that, but his points are clear, concise, unapologetic, and based on research.

That's why, when I was told that Governor Jesse Ventura would appear on ClubWWI.com, I was ecstatic.

At first, I couldn't really believe it. I was told by his representatives that the interview was "definite for April 9th" — but like I've said, in wrestling, there's no such thing as definite. Still a few months away from April at the time, I chalked it up as a definite maybe.

Even when I was sent the phone number to call, I doubted it would really happen.

When I called the number, ten minutes early (as I usually do) and got no answer, I once again figured it would never happen.

So I waited ten minutes before calling back. In the back of my mind I began to formulate what I'd e-mail to the person who set the interview up . . .

Dear Agent Lady,

I called Jesse at 11 a.m. as we discussed and when I did, no one answered the . . .

"Hello?"

"Hi . . . Jesse?"

"Yes. Is this James? Did you call ten minutes ago?"

"Uh . . . yes?"

"Sorry. I was on the phone with another interview. That's why I didn't get it. We're doing these every ten minutes."

That's when I realized that I had Jesse Ventura for only ten minutes. And while ten minutes with the Body is better than an hour with almost anyone else, I still was concerned over how to present such a short discussion to my subscribers. It was an obstacle, but nothing I wasn't familiar with. I remembered the advice of my old sales manager and . . .

Forget all that. This was Jesse Ventura! He was on the phone and we were really going to do this!

"Okay. Just so you know, it's prerecorded. Are you ready?"

Ventura was matter of fact. "You're set for 11. It's 11."

I was so used to wrestlers squirming out at the time of the interview.

"Can we do it tomorrow?"

"Can we do it a week from Friday?"

"Can we do it in November of next year?"

"Can you build a time machine out of scrap metal and we'll do it yesterday?"

So, needless to say, I was thrilled.

Before I talk about our shoot, let me say this — Jesse gave me carte blanche. I could ask anything. I've interviewed former wrestlers, out of the industry for decades, who've told me that certain topics were off-limits. Ventura, a nationally recognized politician, had no such stipulations. I was free to fire at will.

We spent a lot of the interview talking about politics. As I mentioned, I still had a love for the political arena and was, in many ways, amazed that I was able to interview someone who knows the likes of John McCain and the Clintons. When would I have the opportunity again to discuss the pitfalls of the two-party system and sensationalistic news media again? Sure, I had spoken about the pitfalls of CNN's reporting in the wake of the Benoit tragedy with the likes of Steve Blackman and Bill DeMott, but this was something altogether different. Ventura was someone who had to deal with the politics of the media while he was dealing with the politics of, well, politics.

I joked about it right off the bat, by explaining how I usual began interviews by welcoming guests to the Insanity. Since Jesse had spent the week with people like Larry King and Sean Hannity, I said he was probably used to it by now. He laughed and called his media tour a necessary evil when promoting a book. I could only imagine how crazy his week must have been. I mean, the guy had been reamed out by Hannity . . . and Opie and Anthony in the same week. Talk about a strange political spectrum. Given the Body's extreme views, it's understandable that he generates some massive media heat. But what doesn't quite make sense is why they're willing to invite someone on their show, give them a platform, only to scream their own views over him. Why have him there to begin with? After all, it's your show — you can say whatever you want, any day you want.

Okay, maybe that's not entirely true. . . . The Gov explained it to me like this.

> "You watch our news shows now. They're not news shows. They're entertainment shows. I did Sean Hannity and he's trying to tell me they're not told what subjects to talk about, like I said they were, because that's what I went through at MSNBC. So I looked at him off the air and I said, 'So, Sean, it was your call to cover the death of Anna Nicole Smith for a month and a half?'"

I laughed, because Ventura made it all seem so obvious. While others tiptoe around media heavyweights to stay in their good graces, Jess stepped right into the line of fire and reveled. I was impressed by his directness and common sense, and I guess, like many others, I wish I spoke as freely as Ventura. After all, like I've said, that's what the true selling point of our society should be. I told this to Governor Ventura and he agreed.

"Well, let's remember one of our great forefathers, Thomas Jefferson. He was quoted as saying dissention is the greatest form of patriotism. I'll repeat that. Dissention is the greatest form of patriotism. And it troubles me a great deal because I have questions now about 9/11. How can three buildings fall, when only two were hit by airplanes? How can the buildings that fell fall at the rate of gravity if you put a stopwatch on them? If you simply ask these questions today, it seems like you're attacked. Your credibility is attacked and, to use an old Shakespeare quote, they doth protest too much."

I live in New York. On the morning of September 11th, 2001, I was seated at a desk preparing to get to work at my business-to-business sales job. My customers were primarily based in New York, and on that list were countless people in the World Trade Center. I had already started making my calls when the planes had hit. I kept dialing numbers only to be told, "All circuits were busy." It's haunting; I was calling the Twin Towers at the time of the tragedy. When I think back on that day, I remember the phone calls and the names on my list vividly. It's something I'll never forget.

But it's not about agreeing with Jesse Ventura or disagreeing with him. It's about the right to question. It's about being a citizen and investigating the things you don't fully understand or agree with.

Now, if you believe the accepted popular history of September 11th, then you have every right not to raise your hand and speak out. Why would you?

But if you have doubts about anything your government says — be it about taxes, border control, terrorism, election results, or anything else under the red, white, and blue sun — you do have an obligation. If you've lost faith in your elected officials and you keep silent, well, it's just about the most unpatriotic thing you can do. You should not trust in your government because you're afraid; you should trust in your government because there's nothing to make you untrusting.

Ventura was fulfilling his duty as a citizen. At no point in this interview did he try to sway my opinion. In fact, at no point in the interview was my opinion about 9/11 even raised. And no, Jesse didn't come off like someone who was trying to rally anti-American sentiment. He sounded like someone who was deeply pro-American yet trying to reconcile himself with things he didn't fully believe or understand.

To be honest with you, by the time I hung up, I felt more patriotic than I had in years. I felt as though my country's political system was alive and well. In a world of spin and "worked shoots," I had all but given up hope.

But speaking out was nothing new for Ventura. He did it when he was still involved with wrestling; he was politically incorrect before political incorrectness was even invented, before it became a catchphrase used to sell TV shows. He did it behind the mic with Vince McMahon, and it wasn't always pleasant sailing. He told me a story about it, which summed it all up perfectly.

> "Vince was, at times, a great boss to work for. Because, before we went on the mic, he gave me very simple orders. He said, 'If Jesse Ventura believes it, then it's true.' You know, that was my marching orders, to go out there on the mic . . . and that was a brilliant thought, because that allowed me to be me. So he didn't have me out there spinning things. Although, there was one time that he reined me in and we got into a huge fight. Do you remember Koko B. Ware?"

Sure do. Not sure if the Birdman remembers me, though.

> "Okay, well, I came up to Koko one night and I said, 'Koko, I want to make sure you're okay with it.' He said, 'What?' I said, 'I want to say that the B in your name stands for Buckwheat and that you are the grandson of Buckwheat.' Well, Koko looked at me and said, 'Whatever you say, brother. Whatever makes me money, I'm okay with.' So I got his complete approval to do it. Well, when I did it that night, the NAACP came down real hard on McMahon, and he backed down and told me I couldn't do it anymore. And I felt offended over that. You know why? This was the same time that, on *Saturday Night Live*, Eddie Murphy was playing Buckwheat. Remember that? So, in other words, it was

okay for Eddie, because he's black, to make reference to Buckwheat. But it wasn't okay for me to do it, because I'm white. And I had to say, wait a minute . . . *Our Gang*, they were the first integrated family on television. Sure they had their faults, but it was the first time you saw black kids play with white kids on TV. And when they say Buckwheat was a bad stereotype, you're gonna tell me that Alfalfa's the normal white kid? Come on. This is comedy here. If we can't laugh at ourselves, what have we become?"

At this point, Jesse went on to speak about Tito "Chico" Santana and Billy Graham. He seemed happy to be able to discuss the wrestling industry, as opposed to covering the same ground he'd been traversing during his high-profile, whirlwind book tour. He even said, with real excitement in his voice, "You got me talking about wrestling now."

I looked at my watch. We were nearly 30 minutes in. Our ten-minute interview had stretched on for three times its scheduled length. Throughout our talk, I could hear Jesse's call-waiting signal: a brief muted moment signaled that someone else was trying to get their time with the Governor. It also signaled that the Body was ignoring them.

As I was starting to feel guilty for taking so much of his time and about to wrap things up so Ventura could move on to the rest of his media obligations, I knew I'd never forgive myself if I failed to bring up the one wrestling topic I knew he'd have a provocative opinion on — Hulk Hogan.

Like I said, Hogan and Ventura were just about neck and neck when it came to crossover success. For some reason, though, Hulk always seemed to fall short of Jesse's outside-the-ring achievements. I mean, seriously, you can't compare Jess's role in *Predator* to the Hulkster's *Suburban Commando*. And you can't compare Hogan's wrestling publicity stunt presidential campaign with the Body's time in a real Governor's mansion. So it all begged the question: is there professional jealousy on Hulk's part?

"Let me say this. Hogan was the biggest thing ever in wrestling. You know, in our era, there's no doubt about that. Hulkamania and all that. But it's like my agent in Hollywood would say, when everyone was Hulkamania this, Hulkamania that, my agent kept saying, 'Yeah, that's great, but this Jesse Ventura is truly more talented.' Hogan and I have not been on good terms for a long, long time — ever since I tried to unionize wrestling, and he's the one who ratted me to Vince. . . . At that time, I realized this so-called friend was indeed not a friend, that he was completely in it for himself. But that's the nature of the business. You know, it is a cutthroat business, and I accept that. I don't have a great deal of respect for Hogan today, and one of the reasons is because of that show he does, *Hogan Knows Best*. This is just my opinion, but I'd never exploit my family that way. . . . I think that's grasping at stardom and attempting to stay on top."

I knew exactly what he was saying. I am pretty private when it comes to my real life too, and I wouldn't dream of basing a reality show on my family. Each to his own, I guess, but it does seem a bit bizarre. Numerous promotional photos for the series, for example, showed the Hulkster standing next to his scantily clad daughter. Trying to play the role of protective dad, it always seemed forced to me and, well . . . kind of uncomfortable.

And that's just how I put it to Jesse. I said that many felt that pictures of Hulk and Brooke were "uncomfortable."

But Ventura had a better way of saying it.

"He reminds me of a pimp."

I laughed nervously, not sure if he'd really just said that. Okay, sure, it's what I was thinking, and I imagine it was what many others thought too. So I explained to Jess that I was trying to find a nice way to say the same thing when I used the term "uncomfortable." That's when the Governor gave me some of the best advice I think I'll ever get. And although it was something I'd heard him say countless times as a kid, the words took on new meaning . . . because he was saying them directly to me.

"Say it like it is, man!"

You got it, Jesse. Here goes . . .

CHAPTER ELEVEN

WHAT I'M TRYING TO SAY NOW

So, what have I learned? What has changed for me between writing this book and the publication of my first? What does interviewing more than 100 of the most colorful characters from the most misunderstood industry on the face of the planet in a three-year period teach a guy?

Lots.

I've come to realize that we, as fans, can sometimes be too "smart" for our own good. Now, before you jump all over me, hear me out. I'm not saying that we shouldn't be smart in the sense of knowing things about wrestling — we should certainly strive to know as much as possible. It's the same as anything else today. You can't just watch TV anymore — what the stars do behind the scenes has become part of the spectacle. The days of whispers regarding Mr. Brady's spats with producers while his Bunch cowers in fear are over. Now, we know the who, what, where, when, and why of what goes on in the entertainment world almost instantly. Is it good? Not necessarily. Is it bad? Not necessarily. Is it the way it is? Yup.

The issue of wrestling fans' "smartness" getting out of hand comes down to how much stock we put into what we think we know. What we hear about a performer can be based on limited information, half-truths, and sometimes even outright lies. I've dealt with stars who've been maligned for things that they never did. . . . Fans hear a story about a wrestler peeing on a waitress, and from that moment on the wrestler is forever "Waitress Pee-Pee Man." It doesn't mean the story is true — just that fans have heard it. To go out and try to discredit the story often, oddly enough, only serves to make it stronger. Fans believe what they want to believe.

And as Kevin Nash said way back in the first chapter, some wrestlers play into their own mythology. That's the other side of the coin.

The wrestling industry has always been 90% perception. You're supposed to simply believe that a particular star is injured or angry with his opponent. You want to feel the electricity in the air when two wrestlers — embroiled in a vicious feud — meet in the ring. You're supposed to accept, in your heart, that the evil villain is really evil behind the scenes too. . . .

Even when he's not.

You see, fans get worked. Wrestlers get worked. Promoters get worked. Everyone gets worked. It's the nature of professional wrestling. You can't believe or exist in a world based on fantasy and expect to know all the facts of what happens backstage. The reality is that even those who are backstage and experience these things for themselves don't always know. If Bob the Wrestler can't tell whether or not a colleague is truly crazy, how can the fans?

For every story you know about one wrestler, there's about a million you don't know about the others. Wrestlers and fans alike, for example, enjoy sharing a laugh at Pat Patterson jokes. Known just as much for being openly homosexual as he is for being WWE's first Intercontinental Champion, Patterson's legendary. That doesn't mean that he's the only gay man in wrestling — far from it — he's just the one most fans know about.

It all came into focus for me just after the Chris Benoit tragedy. Fans, still making bad jokes about Stone Cold Steve Austin's highly publicized domestic issues, were shocked to find out that the Canadian Crippler had a history of domestic violence as well. Because the police records only became public after the murder-suicide, many wanted to know why they had not heard about it at the time it actually happened. The answer is simple, and everything I just tried to explain to you is true. . . .

There are countless other men who beat their wives, and you never hear about them. Just like there are countless men who love and care for their family who, because of their public persona or demeanor you'd never suspect of having a tender side. Perception means far too much — no matter how "smart" you get, you'll never know everything. That's not just true in pro wrestling — it's true in *life*. Some people are hurt by unfair perceptions; others revel in them — that's the way it is.

I once knew a guy who told people he was in the French foreign legion. I have no idea what it did for him. The only thing I could imagine was that he was a pathological liar.

Oh, wrestling has those too . . .

There's really no black or white in wrestling. We may think we know a grappler based on their rep, but it never represents everything about who they are. I've already covered a number of situations that make this point — Scott Steiner being the biggest example. (No pun intended.) But there are lots more. Consider Buff Bagwell, for example. Sure, I've given him some grief for the insane statements he's made, but there's more to him than just that. When I was setting up his interview, I asked him to be sure not to forget, and he said, "No problem. You're in my calendar. You don't know me, but ask anyone who does. If you're in my calendar, you're good to go. I'll be there."

Sure enough, he was. And again, that's something beyond rare in wrestling. It's also a side of Buff that few know, and something that would probably surprise a lot of his detractors. We, as fans, often lose sight of the fact that these people aren't just stories and stereotypes. They're individuals, just like us, and they all have many layers and aspects to their personalities. Speaking of which . . .

I admit, I've also learned that not everything is about me. That sounds silly when I read it back to myself, but it's true. People who write about a business or industry for a while tend to take things . . . to heart. When you're a baseball journalist and argue the teams should offer better ticket prices, you can't help but feel that the company listened to your advice when they eventually slash costs for the fans — even if it happens two years later.

It's even worse when you're talking about professional wrestling. Maybe it's because of the whole work vs. reality thing that we tend to read so much into every single statement, but clearly, not everything a wrestler says during a promo is a tongue-in-cheek reference to something else. If Randy Orton comes out and says, "Tonight I want a match with John Cena," it's not because he's making a veiled reference to something that happened backstage *last* night. Ninety-nine percent of the time, it's just a statement, something that deserves no further analysis. Yet fans have a habit of analyzing everything to death.

I've had that happen with things I've written. People have picked apart my articles only to find hidden meanings — things that just weren't there. Now keep in mind, I'm much more accessible than Vincent Kennedy McMahon. If people can find meaning that isn't there in things I've written, imagine what the big wrestling companies go through.

And yes, I've been guilty of this, too. I was especially guilty when I wrote my first book — and I was guilty of it for a long time before that. Fans and the wrestling media want to believe that there are ten layers to everything, because that gives us something to analyze and debate. There's nothing fun about picking apart something that's mono-dimensional — better to construct conspiracies, convince yourself that your theories are true, and hammer away at every lead you think you've found.

Even now, I'm sure there are people who will read this and think I'm talking about a particular person or wrestling media entity. But I'm not; this isn't a shot at the *Torch*, the *Observer*, *PWInsider*, *Figure Four*, or any other wrestling news site. I'm simply saying that it's something that I realize I was guilty of at one time.

I also think I understand Bob Holly and all the locker room self-policing he's been associated with a bit better now too. In *World Wrestling Insanity* I was particularly brutal toward Bob's public beatdown of Rene Dupree for violating one of wrestling's unwritten backstage codes of conduct. While I still stand by the fact that things like that should not spill into the ring, I understand the need for people like Holly now, much better, at least, than I did just a few years ago. In a business of big guys with big muscles and big egos, some performers can only understand and respect redress when it occurs, violently, from their peers. It's part of the nature of such a physical business. Looking back on high school, for example, wouldn't you be more likely to see the captain of the football team push around a non-performing teammate than the captain of the math team?

Is it a tool that management uses to keep the guys pitted against each other? Sure. Was it created for that purpose? No. It was created because there's some "tough guys" who can't be made to understand in any other way. It's sad but it's true, and I get that now.

Something else I've learned (and it's something that won't win me many new fans, but whatever, Jesse said to tell it like it is) is that the minutiae of wrestling's history really doesn't matter all that much.

Sure, okay, it matters if you're writing about history or researching an issue. But for the most part, the wrestlers themselves don't even bother to remember. I've interviewed stars who've forgotten the promoters they've worked for, who've mixed up the dates of major events, and who even willfully omit huge parts of their own autobiography. The amazing thing is that some people will make you feel like less of a fan for not knowing when a wrestler won a title — when, chances are, the wrestler doesn't even remember himself. In all my time doing this, my knowledge of wrestling history has come in handy for just one thing — helping guests who may have forgotten a name.

"I would have loved to work with Gorgeous George . . ."

"George Wagner?"

"Yeah, George Wagner."

"I worked for an old guy in Oregon. Oh geez . . . what the hell's his name?"

"Don Owen?"

"Yeah, Don Owen."

My personal favorite was when Bushwhacker Luke spoke about the people he met at a recent TNA show: "Kurt Angle and the colored fellow from WWE. What's his name?"

"Uh . . . Booker T?"

"Yeah, Booker T."

Oh-kay . . .

Alright, sure, it might also help you in random trivial pursuits. You know who won the opening match of the December 10, 1981, NWA Power Hour show — great. If you happen to be on *Jeopardy* and Alex Trebek happens to introduce the category "Extremely Obscure Crap From NWA History," you're in the money. If not, then I'm not sure what the point of being able to rattle it all out is. It never impressed me much, and it impresses me even less now.

Wrestling is actually about a much bigger picture, and it's more interesting to try to understand why things worked, or didn't, so that you can avoid making the mistakes of the past or try to recreate success in the future. You desperately need to know the general concepts, but sometimes getting bogged down in details only hurts your understanding of what's truly important: you can't see the forest for the trees.

Let me put it to you like this. A successful TV producer doesn't need to know the name of the person who played Timmy's teacher on *Lassie*. But he sure as hell better know that *Lassie* was a show about a dog that saved people trapped in wells.

When I need to look up a date or match listing from the past, I most certainly do so. There are plenty of writers out there who specialize in wrestling history, and many do a great job. In fact, we have our own personal wrestling historian, Mike Rickard, who does that for World Wrestling Insanity. Books and websites exist to make it easier for you to find that kind of info at the drop of a hat. There's no need for fans to commit it to memory and recite it just to sound like you know a lot of things. I mean, seriously, who does it impress? The people on a message board? The people in a Facebook group? The people in line at the concession stand at a freakin' house show?

Admit it, we've all been there and had to deal with that guy. Nothing makes waiting to buy a hot dog any less fun than listening to a chronological rundown of Sabu's first 100 matches. And if it bugs us so much, imagine how it sounds to a wrestler. . . .

Rather than tell me where and when Adrian Adonis and Dick Murdoch won the WWF Tag Team Title, explain what made them so special that they deserved it — that'll impress me, reciting from the back of a baseball card won't. Hell, you can make a Teddy Ruxpin doll do that. Memorization doesn't mean you understand something — it just means you've committed something to memory.

I guess what I'm really saying is that I've learned not to take myself too seriously. Like I said, I'm not curing cancer — I'm aware of that. Sure, it's great to pat myself on the back and say that everything I'm doing is of the utmost importance — but clearly, it's not.

That doesn't mean that I think what I do is irrelevant. I'll always remember the joy I felt when I first learned about Vince Russo's radio show on Long Island. I think about how I'd stay up until 3 a.m. on Saturday night, pull my clock radio under the covers, and listen to WFAN's wrestling broadcast low enough so that no one in my house would wake up. I remember sinking countless quarters into payphones so that I could call Coach Kurt's 976 wrestling line. If I can evoke just some of those feelings in fans today, that's enough for me.

I don't need to be changing the world; I just need to know that what I do makes some folks happy or helps them forget about their troubles for a while. Feeling like I bring them closer to the stars they love puts a smile on my face.

At the end of the day, I make no bones about the fact that I think I have the best job on the planet. I love what I do and, as I hope I've made clear throughout this book, I can't imagine going back and telling myself at a young age that I would get the opportunity to share and learn so much with the people I have interviewed.

I've asked Bobby Eaton about his famous Scaffold Match. I've talked with Road Warrior Animal about his early days with Hawk. I've heard stories from Million Dollar Man about debuting on WWF TV and bringing new meaning to the term villain. That, to me, is priceless. And I can honestly say that if I had to stop tomorrow I wouldn't feel that there are things I'd regret or left undone.

I have my listeners and the readers to thank for that. Without them, I'm just a dude with a digital recorder bugging random people. What started out as an obligation to other wrestling fans turned into a dream come true, and I appreciate the opportunity more than you can ever know.

Okay, enough. It's time for the shocking revelation, the big close. Are you ready for it? The biggest thing I learned since the last book . . . the most surprising revelation . . . the thing that I never, ever, saw coming.

Take a deep breath . . .

Vince McMahon and World Wrestling Entertainment care about wrestling and they treat employees well.

What? I know, I know! Like *Through the Looking Glass*, ain't it? I mean . . . what the?

In my first book I blasted the entire promotion for every misstep they made. As I mentioned at the start of all this, I felt it was deserved, and to some extent, I still do. After all, the period I was focusing on was pretty terrible. In fact, right before I started writing about wrestling, I nearly stopped watching. For the first time in my life, I was ready to give it all up. I'm not sure I ever spoke about that publicly, but it's true.

The whole thing might sound stupid, but hear me out. In 2002, WWE presented an angle where Shawn Michaels was attacked in a parking lot on *Raw*. As usual, the entire story was shaped as a whodunit. We were all supposed to have our suspects, and we were invited to try to figure out who the culprit really was.

I'd had my fill of this kind of mystery angle back in 1999 when, leading up to the Survivor Series PPV, Steve Austin had been hit by a car. At that time, the only clue fans had was that the culprit had blond hair. Triple H swore it wasn't him. I hoped it was Chris Jericho. But no, as it turns out, it was Rikishi. The dancing, big-bottomed Samoan had turned bad and, although it wasn't the best pay-off in the world, at least it wasn't Triple H . . .

Except that it was. A few weeks later, it came out that Hunter was behind everything. Ho-hum. It always seemed to be The Game who masterminded everything and it started to suck the fun out of these mysteries. Hell, what is there to figure out if the answer is always the same? It's like a game show where every answer is "four." How long can you watch that?

Well, in the 2002 attack on Shawn Michaels, Helmsley once

again promised us he was innocent. But even as the words left his lips, I knew it wasn't true. After all, I had fallen for this before. . . .

When the two-hour show came to a close, the camera zoomed in and revealed a pixilated security cam image of the culprit to be — dum, dum, *dum* — Triple H.

And though I wanted to kick myself in the face for sitting through that episode of *Raw*, it had nothing to do with Hunter. It could have been anyone else and I would have felt the same. The wrestling that I'd loved for years had become a shell of its former self. It was predictable. It was tiresome. And, thanks to a family member in wrestling trunks, it had become a one-man show. Yeah, it really is pretty boring when the answer to every question is Hunter Hearst Helmsley.

So, then and there, I decided to stop watching WWE programming. I would, instead, simply check websites and read results to get my wrestling fix. That's what I did for a few weeks and, because of my newfound familiarity with internet reports, I found a job posting looking for a wrestling writer. . . .

I definitely had a grudge heading into all this. After all, I had come close to giving up something I loved because of how stale WWE TV had become. I made it my mission to explain that to others. And the first book was just that: it began the month after I vowed to stop watching and ended with the feud that started things back in the right direction — Triple H vs. Batista.

Okay, I don't want to take back the entire book. I'm proud of it and, although I wish I could erase some of its snarkiness, I was glad to say my piece. But now, years later, I'm able to see things in a different light. No longer taking things too seriously, getting bogged down in small details, or believing half-truths spun by someone else, I'm able to relate to you how I've come to understand World Wrestling Entertainment — from the people who worked there.

For the most part, the people who have worked for Vince McMahon actually *like* Vince McMahon. That, my friends, is called a fact. Sure, there are some folks who don't, but 99 times out of 100, a star has nothing but praise for Vince — even if they have a negative view of the company itself. He leads by example (something I did give him credit for in *World Wrestling Insanity)*, but he also clearly cares about his employees. I could fill 200 pages with quotes from the stars who have undying respect for the chairman. Seriously.

Vince McMahon interviews Greg Valentine

Again, forget the ingrained cynicism and look at the whole picture. And no, it's not just because people are kissing Vince's butt. How do I know? Because those same people aren't so quick to jump on the Triple H bandwagon. Stars who have given me glowing reviews of VKM's benevolence have turned around and crucified the self-proclaimed King of Kings with their very next sentence. If they were truly looking to angle their way into a job, they surely wouldn't be publicly insulting the boss's son-in-law, right?

Hell, I have yet to interview a single person who's had a positive story to tell about Johnny "Ace" Laurinaitis, one of the company's vice presidents. Successful butt kissing requires kissing all the right butts. Not just the biggest one.

Look at Kid Kash. Here's a guy who was ready to burn down the TNA offices while he was there. He not only hit them below the belt, he shot at them with a freakin' machine gun. But listen to what he had to say about WWE: "One thing about WWE, buddy. They are the most professional, put-together, well-organized company that I have ever worked for in my entire life. You know? They're the real deal, man."

And yup, he was talking about a company that had just released him. It means a lot when someone like Kash gives you an endorsement like that.

Or how about Terry Funk? Here's a guy that stands for everything

WWE isn't. He turned down an initial offer to join Vince's ECW reincarnation that would have made him good money — when you think of corporate politics, you don't think of Terry. However, despite their philosophical differences, the Funker has respect for McMahon, the employer, and what he offers those who work for him.

> "Truth of the matter is that I can sit here and talk about WWE, but let me tell you something, they've made a lot of guys millionaires. Do I approve of what their product [is]? Not really . . . Do I approve of the way he treats his talent? Yes, I do. He treats them very well. But I don't really approve of the product he produces, you know? The one thing about wrestling before is that even Terry Funk, even anybody, it didn't matter who it was, you didn't like what somebody was saying, the money wasn't right . . . For whatever reason it might be, you could go ahead and pick up your bag, walk out that door, get in your car, and go to another part of the country and go to work. And now you can't do that. That's where the big difference is in wrestling then and wrestling now. Are [today's wrestlers] more fortunate? Yes, they are. Do they have more people who will be able to retire and live their life after wrestling? Yes . . . Would I rather life in that era or this one? I'll take the other one."

So no, clearly, everything isn't black or white. But you don't have to love WWE's direction to respect how they do business.

In the end, I was simply wrong. Just as many fans are wrong in the way they perceive certain wrestlers, I was wrong in the way I looked at WWE as a whole. Are they the greatest company ever to exist in any industry? Of course not. Are they pretty damn good at what they do and how they care for their workers? You betcha. The list of former employees, even those who left on bad terms, with fond memories for the company, reads like a who's who. Other promotions can't say the same thing, that's for sure.

Released TNA stars simply don't offer the same love and admiration for their former company. I would never have expected that just a few years ago, but it's a fact.

It was actually when I began defending the McMahons during the Benoit tragedy that I finally realized how my attitude had changed. While so many tried to lynch Vince for the horrors perpetuated by one performer, I couldn't but feel for the man. It all seemed . . . *insane* to me. How could people have such a terrible view of the guy? The conversations I had both privately and publicly with former WWE employees had taught me that the boss wasn't that bad. Sure, he's no Mr. Rogers, but he's not Dr. Evil either.

Vince McMahon, WWE Chairman

And then I realized that had the tragedy occurred just two years earlier, I would have probably been right there in line with the rest of the mob screaming for McBlood. It made me a bit sick inside, and I was embarrassed by how much anger I'd once harbored for someone I only knew from his public persona. It's an industry where guys like Kevin Nash relish in misconceptions about their true nature, and Vince had clearly done so too. Unfortunately, and because of this, many viewed him as nothing more than a caricature. It finally became clear to me, and though I was shocked to find myself jumping to WWE's defense, there was no other choice.

Just a few years ago, I believed World Wrestling Entertainment was a mad house where wrestlers cried in corners while Mr. McManson tossed poisoned daggers at them. Now, I see things quite differently. The weirdest thing about all this?

I couldn't be happier to be wrong.

As I've said many times, we're talking about a wrestling organization I've always loved. We're talking about a business I've always loved. Sadly, my "smarts" had affected my ability to enjoy wrestling as entertainment for a long, long time. I looked at WWE as an evil corporation and the wrestlers as hapless carnies who would stab you in the back for a dollar. My cynicism kept something I truly loved as a child from being something I could also love as an adult.

The irony, of course, is that it was the wrestling industry itself, and the people in it, that gave it all back to me. It was the performers' stories, my interaction with wrestlers, and hearing first-hand accounts about backstage issues that showed me I had nothing to be disillusioned about. . . . The guy who once thought he had the entire business figured out realized that he didn't.

In fact, I still haven't figured it out. I could do a thousand more interviews and still never be able to figure out professional wrestling.

And that's why I love it.

CHAPTER TWELVE

. . . QUESTIONS LATER

Like the title says, the questions come later. Well, it's later. And what are some of the things that listeners have asked most often over the years?

How about: What do you like best about doing these interviews? I've already mentioned how I truly enjoy the fact that I'm able to bring performers, as the people they really are, to wrestling fans. But what I haven't talked about is how proud I am that I can keep up my end of the conversation with wrestling's legends. There's nothing cooler than hearing Harley Race say, "It's just like *you* said, earlier . . ."

Ole Anderson notwithstanding, I still marvel at the fact that guys like Dory Funk Jr., The Valiant Brothers, Bruno Sammartino, Ivan Koloff, and Nick Bockwinkel have come to ClubWWI and haven't said, "Yo, stop. Do you even know what you're talking about?" And I have to admit, at times I've expected that.

And then there's: Who is the nicest wrestler you ever interviewed? Jimmy Hart is not only one of the coolest people I've met in the wrestling business, but one of the nicest people I've met in my life. There is no one in wrestling as widely appreciated, liked, and employed as The Mouth of the South. Talking to Jimmy for all of a minute automatically puts you in a good mood. He answers the phone like he's singing a Gentrys tune. When he hangs up, he says, "I love you, baby" — and it's not creepy. It's like Jimmy Hart was plucked from a 1950s Memphis recording studio and parachuted into pro wrestling.

The Mouth of the South

I once called Jimmy and he carried on with the conversation for a few minutes, cheery as always. Then, when I asked how things were by him, he told me he was waiting to hear some important news on a family member fighting in Iraq following an assault that morning. Had he not told me, I'd never have known — that's just how he is. You'd be hard pressed to find too many people with something negative to say about Jimmy.

Others have wanted to know: Which guest were you most surprised by? Mae Young takes the cake. When I called Mae for the 100th "Radio Free Insanity" show, I had no idea what to expect; I had never spoken to her before. Even stranger, I had never really talked to anyone about her. She just never came up. I had, of course, dealt with many people who'd worked with her, and I'd talked to guests like Eric Bischoff and Ivory about experiences with her on television, but I never asked anyone what she was like behind the scenes. I just assumed she was, well, her character. (For those that don't know, the elderly diva is known on television for being incoherent, sex-obsessed, and half-insane.)

In reality, Mae Young is a very sweet woman with a wealth of wrestling experiences — a resume rivaling anyone in the business today. She was articulate and amazing as a guest. There aren't many people who can tell you a story about Ed "Strangler" Lewis and inform you that they're scheduled to fight Triple H's daughter in the same interview. I was happy to have her on and proud of what turned out to be a great interview with a woman WWE would induct into the Hall of Fame just a few months later.

Then there's the dreaded: What's your worst interview ever? Some people expect me to say Dave Hebner, who, during each of his two shoots, had what can only be described as tunnel vision about the

WWE VP, Johnny Laurinaitis, who fired him. Everything for Dave came back to Johnny Law-nye-tus: What was your favorite match? The one where John Law-nye-tus gets eaten by a bear. What's your favorite movie? The *John Law-nye-tus Is a Maggot* movie.

That's pretty much how it went. But no, Dave wasn't my least favorite interview. In fact, I actually liked speaking with him. Sure, everything came back to the same subject, but at least it gave me something to work with. When I sent out the press release on Dave, I knew that Johnny Law-nye-tus was the perfect buzzword.

Ernest Miller, now that's a different story. I hated that interview. From start to finish, it was . . . doomed. The Cat, out in L.A., seemed like he was in the middle of a house party when I called. The interview even included a few minutes on the phone with his agent . . . I just went along for the ride.

To give you an idea of how excruciating it was, I need only point to the way he answered one question. I asked Ernest about dancing with James Brown at WCW's Superbrawl 2000. Usually, when a guest did something big like this, I simply have to say, "Tell me about . . ." and then go from there. If they bitchslapped William Shatner, tossed a midget, or won a World Title, those three magic words, "tell me about," get you a great story, every time.

Except in this case. Miller responded with, "Well, did you see it?"

I told him I had, and then he said, "Well, there you go. You probably just stopped dancing now."

That's it. That was his answer. Yeah, Ernest Miller was a . . . tough sell.

Some people have also wondered: Do you pay for interviews? Nope, never have. I've been asked to on a few occasions, but the guys who asked for money weren't the ones I would even consider paying. I'm a media outlet, not a wrestling promoter. I give my guests a chance to speak to fans, and I promote whatever they have coming up through press releases and site announcements. For a wrestler, it's a chance to generate some buzz, clear up false rumors, and speak directly to the people who care most about their career. I've spoken to hundreds of performers and, in total, maybe five have asked me for money.

Honestly? It surprises me too. When I first started doing this, I expected many more to expect even a nominal payday. It's just another in the long line of misconceptions about wrestling that I've had cleared up during the run of my show.

What about technical problems? You already read about the Scott Steiner incident, but what you're about to read was even more embarrassing. And it's not even about technical issues with the show per se. It's about my phone.

In October 2007, WWE's website reported that Mike "Corporal" Kirschner had passed away. Where they got this from, no one's quite sure. All we know is that Mike wasn't dead. Thanks to an article by Greg Oliver of *SLAM! Wrestling,* the cat was out of the bag. The Corporal was alive.

I interviewed Mike that next week and he found humor in the misreported (and never corrected) WWE story. Now a truck driver, Kirschner acknowledged the crazy situation with a joke of his own: "I'm hearing, 'Hey man. You're dead.' I'm not dead. My career might be, but I'm not!"

Now, here's where the technical problem comes in. When I called Mike I was at home, rather than my office. I hooked up the recorder and pushed the buttons that I believed would turn off my call waiting. I've done it a million times and it's never been a problem. You just press *70 and call.

Unfortunately, I didn't get all the numbers right. Later, I discovered I'd dialed *73 by accident before calling Mike.

Wanna know what *73 does?

Well, for starters, it doesn't turn off call waiting. Secondly, it forwards all your incoming calls to the next number you enter.

And what number was that? Um, yeah, the recently undead Cpl. Kirschner's . . .

It wasn't all that long before my cell phone rang. It was my wife.

"Hi. Who the heck is Michael from North Carolina, and why is he answering our phone?"

Another thing people are curious about is whether I've ever had a guest end an interview badly. And well, the answer to that is not really, not in an abrupt manner. I've had guests tell me when they had to go, and I've had some mention we'd been going on too long, but no one's ever just hung up because I offended them.

Now, the award for the most imaginative way anyone ever told me they wanted to end our discussion has to go to Juventud Guerrera. Known as the Juice in WCW and WWE, Juvi is also known for his wild lifestyle and broken English. I had always been a fan of the Juice, and was really thrilled when he agreed to do an interview.

About 15 minutes in, after a question that had nothing to do with dinner or Sean "X-Pac" Waltman, he answered by telling me he actually had company in a way that only the Juice could: "I was just talking with Sean. X-Pac that is, right in front of me. X-Pac in Mexico and, uh, we are just having dinner here . . . But anyways . . ."

It took me two minutes, literally, to figure out what he was talking about. Juve was in the middle of eating, and he wanted to go. When I finally figured this out, I finished things up and thanked him for the interview which, despite its abrupt end, turned out better than you'd imagine given the language barrier.

And, of course, conflicting dinner schedules.

Another surprisingly popular question? What was the Iron Sheik like off-air? Well . . . the same as Iron Sheik on-air. For the most part, Khosrow Vasiri is a nice, laid-back guy. In fact, 90% of the interview consists of "That is very intelligent question you ask me" and "I had much respect for Mr. So-and-so." It's only when you hit one of his hot buttons that he goes nuts. If my name had been B. Brian Blair, however, I think I'd be telling you a different story.

The real gist of this question is whether or not the Sheik is a work. After all, his craziness is so legendary it's caused Howard Stern endless enjoyment. Most people simply can't believe that he really is the way he is.

To be honest, I think he is . . . somewhat. The Iron Sheik

reminded me of the type of kid we all gathered around in school. He'd get worked up and start freaking out about something, and then everyone would egg him on until he got more and more out of control. Then he'd throw something at the teacher or jump off the school's roof.

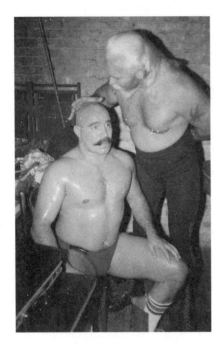

The Iron Sheik and "Handsome" Johnny Valiant

And that's Sheik in a nutshell. He's big on respect and honor, and he has a short fuse. When he starts becoming angry, there's no stopping him. Realizing that people enjoy hearing him like that, why would he bother reining himself in? Think about it. If you knew that you could go buck silly — yelling and screaming and frothing at the mouth — and that people would enjoy it, even pay to see it, would you stop? Would you go to anger management or switch to decaf? Hell no!

Me, personally? I'd go insane every chance I got!

I'd break your back! I'd make you humble! I'd fuc . . .

Uh, hang on. Maybe I wouldn't do everything that Sheik does. But I'd do most of it. Definitely. Definitely the first two . . .

This, I guess, leads to the question: Are there guests you regret having on? Funny enough — no. While some interviews were better than others, I think everyone gave me something decent to share with the listeners. Of course, there was the Ernest Miller thing . . .

I do wish, however, that some of my early guests had come on later instead. A.J. Styles, Samoa Joe, Rhino, and Chris Daniels, for example, are guys I would have loved to spoken to once I had some more experience. While those interviews were quite ranging, they didn't have the same conversational feel that the later shows feature.

I also wouldn't have asked them so many dumb questions . . . I still shudder at some of those.

So yeah, go ahead. Ask.

Did you ever ask a question you wish you could take back? Yes. There are many, but one in particular will always stand out. When I was interviewing Christopher Daniels, a star performer for TNA and ROH, I drew a blank. With nothing to follow up on, I asked him about a match he had . . . ten years earlier . . . in WCW . . . where he fell on his head.

Worse, it had a terrible follow-up too. Something like, "What do you think at a moment like that?"

Almost everyone has their own variation of this one: Have you ever thought about having [insert wrestler here] on? Yes.

I know what you're thinking: Yeah, but what about . . . ? Him too. If someone has been with WWE, TNA, or WCW, I've most likely reached out to them or, at the very least, thought about getting them on. At the end of the day, I probably try to contact five people for every one that I manage to get for the show. Some I never find numbers on; some I never connect with; some agree and then play an endless game of Catch Me If You Can.

Chances are, if you've thought about them, so have I. Of course, some I try harder to reach than others. In the end, those that I've set my sights on usually find their way to the site.

My wife once asked me if I ever worry about running out of people to interview, but the beauty of it all is, that's impossible. I could do ten interviews a day for years and still have a list of people who've never appeared.

Finally, there's my favorite question: Who were you most surprised you were able to get? Jesse Ventura is the obvious choice, I guess, in terms of larger-than-life guests. Eric Bischoff, Jerry Lawler, Mae Young — they all fit that bill too. There's one guy who surprised me, however, for much different reasons.

Fred "Shockmaster/Tugboat/Typhoon" Ottman was a huge deal to me, okay? He wasn't main-eventing WWE pay-per-views in 2008, so it's not that. I desperately wanted to get him was because, well, he literally fell on his face in a WCW debut that has since become the stuff of legend. I never expected to get to Ottman. The Shockmaster had become a running joke in wrestling circles — to the point that fans didn't even consider him "real" anymore.

I tried everything I could think of to find Ottman, but nothing worked. Then, one day, out of the blue, I was on the phone with a promoter and mentioned how I'd love to someday interview Typhoon. I said it in a way that implied I accepted that it would never happen. And that's when he said, "Oh, Fred. I just talked to him. Do you want his number?"

Fred Ottman: Tugboat, Typhoon, Shockmaster

Hell's yeah, I want his number!

When the interview finally happened I was able to put a voice to the fabled Shockmaster story. Ottman spoke at length about why it happened and I learned what it was like to deal with the aftermath. The irony? Fred was now a safety inspector in Florida. Talk about making up for past sins.

CHAPTER THIRTEEN

WHO WOULD YOU . . . ?

After more than 100 interviews, there's one question in my arsenal that's remained pretty much standard.

"If you could choose to wrestle anyone, maybe someone you grew up watching, maybe someone who wrestled after you left, or someone you never crossed paths with — someone who made you say, 'I wish I could have worked with *him* . . .' — who would you pick and why?"

It's pretty straightforward, I know, but it's elicited more amazing responses than I could have ever hoped for. The question simply brings out the fan in everyone. From young stars like Idol Stevens to established legends like Dory Funk Jr., everyone pauses to think about someone they respect. It gives you a real insight into what makes wrestlers and wrestling tick.

As time passed, the question became my interview-closer — right before I gave the subject a chance to speak directly to his or her fans. It took a few shoots for me to figure out that I should add it to the regular schedule, however, and because of this, what you're about to read is missing a few names. Still, the words of more than 100 of wrestling's top stars will follow.

Just so you know, when I first began asking what seems like a standard, simple question, I actually discovered a problem with how, exactly, to put it. The key is in the phrase "work with." Before I realized that was the best way to structure the question, I asked things like "make money with" or "have a good match with," and at times that caused some confused responses. It wasn't until I settled on "work with" that guests were truly comfortable enough to answer clearly. Wrestling you see, despite being an often brutal, physical art form, is also a business of subtlety and nuance . . . and besides, each person has his or her own reason for wanting to work with someone. It might be to have a good match. Or it might be to make a lot of money. Either way, it's up to them.

Finally, I want to make it clear that I really do ask this question to every single guest. I don't shy away from certain stars because they've "worked with everyone." Sure, I hear that a lot: "Oh man . . .What a question! I've worked with everyone." But once a guest says that they inevitably stop, think, and then come up with a thoughtful answer. In almost every case, it's a name I would never have guessed.

There's something amazing about interviewing someone who says they wished they could have wrestled Bruno Sammartino — and then interviewing Bruno and getting to hear his answer. It's like one question brings generations of wrestlers together, and it truly helps you understand what it is about wrestling that *wrestlers* love. The bottom line is this: a guy can talk until he's blue in the face about what he likes or doesn't like about the business. But it's when he names someone he respects, someone he'd love to want to work with above all others, that his real take on the business comes into perspective.

So, read on. Chances are, you'll do what I did . . . and picture some of the best wrestling matches the world will ever see.

Mr. Hughes: I've pretty much worked with all of them. The Funk brothers. Harley Race. Ric Flair. I've pretty much worked with the guys I grew up watching. Junkyard Dog, you know, Rufus R. Jones. People like that. So there's nobody new I'd want to work with outside of those guys I just mentioned.

Erik Watts: That's a tough one because you have to remember I was raised in the business. . . . I would want to wrestle — and I know this sounds stupid — my father. I want to know what those people were going through because I know my dad's intensity — and it's his way or the highway. I would want to know what it would be like to be Bobby Fulton for one night, where it's like this is what we're doing; this is where we're going. And call it in the ring. Because he was a genius in the ring.

Samu: I would say The Rock and A.J. Styles. . . . The same reason. I think I could have a great, great match with them. Different kind of matches, of course.

Mike Bucci: Just for entertainment purposes, as Simon Dean, I would have said Gorgeous George. I think a Simon Dean-Gorgeous George match would have been pretty funny. As Nova, I would have said probably an early '90s (Jushin) Liger or Dynamite Kid. But you know, I've got to throw Shawn in there too. I never got to do anything with Shawn Michaels. . . . I think he clotheslined me in a Royal Rumble one time, over the top rope . . . that I think I got paid, like, four grand for. . . .

Big Daddy V

Big Daddy V: Abdullah the Butcher or Andre the Giant. One of those two. . . . I actually did get a chance to wrestle Abdullah in Puerto Rico. He took the Universal Title away from me and I'm telling you, man . . . there was blood everywhere. It was fascinating to wrestle Abby, man, because he was one of a kind.

The Honky Tonk Man: I only had one match with Harley Race. I wish I would have had more matches with him. I never had a match with Dory Funk Jr. or with Terry or with Captain Redneck Dick Murdoch. He was such a comedian and the way he did stuff was so great. I only had one match with Jack Brisco; I wish I would have had more. The one I loved having matches with the most — I didn't get very many — was, of course, with Hogan. Because when you got that legdrop, it was worth $10,000.

J.J. Dillon: There's more than one. I met Gorgeous George one time and that was towards the end of his career. It would have been exciting to see Gorgeous George and maybe be in his corner when he was in his prime. I'm also a big fan of Japanese wrestling. I know that Rikidozan was the father of wrestling in Japan and though I had met his sons . . . it would have been great at one time to have actually met Rikidozan.

"Nasty Boy" Brian Knobbs: I would have liked to have a real, real match with the Hulkster, I really would. I was in the Royal Rumble with him . . . We were the last three in there, me, Earthquake, and Hulkster. Hulk gave me the big boot over the top rope and I didn't even touch the top rope. I was so excited. But I would love to have a match with him and whoever would have been his partner. I would have loved to wrestle him single, but even in a tag team. Anything. Just to have that experience, because, let's face it . . . he's the Elvis of wrestling. He tore the roof off the place every night, you know?

Jumpin' Jim Brunzell: "I was very fortunate to work with Dory Funk and Terry Funk. Never got an opportunity to work with Jack Brisco, who was a wonderful, wonderful worker and a great champion. I worked with Bob Orton, who I consider one of the best, if not the best, for his style. He was a great, great worker. Oh, Flair too. Right now, I don't know, because there's such contrasting styles . . . I'd probably want to pick somebody I could wrestle and make a lot of money. So whoever the champion is. And I don't know how many champions they have now in the WWE; there's a number of them. You know, the young Orton boy would be fun because I had unbelievable matches with Bob Orton. . . . I'm glad to see that his son has done so well.

Baron Von Raschke: I'm perfectly happy the way I am. I worked with all the great ones: Bruno Sammartino, Verne Gagne, Pat Patterson, Bobo Brazil. There's just so many really, really great ones. During my time, I don't think I missed too many of them. If I did, I'm sorry. I'm perfectly happy working in my garden and doing little carpentry projects for my kids. Playing with my grand[kids]. So I can't worry about wrestling a fictional match with a fictional opponent. When people ask me my toughest match, I always say, my next one.

Bruno "Harvey Wippleman" Lauer: It's funny, I can't really give you an answer to that one, because I'm satisfied with what I've done in the biz. Who I managed, who I traveled with. I really have to say there's nobody. There might be situations . . . I wish I could have had more input . . . in booking a little bit. Maybe in Memphis. Maybe I wished I would have stayed in Kansas City a little longer and refereed. Maybe Bob Geigel would have let me help with the booking then . . . I think the biggest thing I could say is — which is kind of a cop out, but I don't want to make something up just for the sake of it — the guys that I managed that I liked a lot and never made it to the level I wish they would have . . . was the Batten Twins. They were ahead of their time. If they were in their prime, I'd guarantee they'd be in WWE and would be a top tag team.

Bryan Clark: Stan Hansen, absolutely. When [Kronik] won the belts in Japan, he's the one who presented us the belts. I've got a big poster of that in my office. He was a guy I absolutely loved to watch . . . I mean, he just kicked ass. He was brutal on his opponents and he was just one of my favorites.

Terri Runnels: This is easy because I just loved — I thought he was wonderful, he was fun backstage, fun during a match when I worked opposite him — and that was Shawn Michaels. He and I are friends. I always respected him. But I think his work is . . . impeccable. My idea would have something where Dustin was mistreating me as Goldust. And [Shawn], being a chivalrous, top-ranking soul, would have come to my rescue and I would have gone with him for a while and done some angles with him. I loved the way he worked. That would have been one person I would have loved to work with that I never got the chance to.

Scotty 2 Hotty: Probably Hulk Hogan. I never got to do anything with him. I met him a few times when he came around towards the end of his WWE days. To be honest, I wasn't a Hulk Hogan fan as a kid. But as I got older and I learned more about the business — timing and all that — I learned to appreciate it more. He'd always pop in at the right time and leave at the right time. There were guys like Shawn Michaels and Owen Hart. Those were the guys that I always name as guys I look up to and model myself after I think, as a wrestler. But I wrestled Owen a number of times. I actually wrestled Shawn Michaels once. I would like to have another match with Shawn Michaels at one point. That would be great, because he was it for me growing up. But as far as someone I've never done anything with? Hulk Hogan.

Dawn Marie: Miss Elizabeth. I never even got a chance to meet her. As a fan, I wish I would have been able to meet her. I wish I would have been able to work with Captain Lou. I was able to meet Sherri Martel . . . very nice lady, very knowledgeable. She gave me a lot of knowledge. We sat down one day and talked about life and family and choices we make in the business. It helped me a lot through a phase. Who would I work with? I would definitely say them. Captain Lou is a wonderful man. I definitely steal a lot of my stuff from Lou.

Rikishi: There's so many greats out there and I've worked with so many of them. I probably would have liked to work with Bruiser Brody. The reason why I say that is because our style is kind of rugged. Kind of snug. . . . And I always liked how Bruiser Brody would come in there and kick ass. I always thought I would have liked to experience mixing it up with the great Bruiser Brody. Bless his heart. I know he was one of the greats in our industry. So Rikishi's answer would have to be Bruiser Brody.

Paul Roma: I never watched wrestling before I got in it. Believe that one or not, it's the truth. I was approached to get into wrestling. I think the only thing I would have wanted to try would have been the steel cage match. I've never wrestled in a steel cage. But other than that — nobody. I wrestled everyone I wanted to wrestle. And I've wrestled a lot of people I didn't want to wrestle 'cause they were just so bad.

Rick Martel: Wow, that's a pretty tough question. There's so many great wrestlers around these days. I got to see, in fact, *WrestleMania* [XXIV]. Man, I hadn't watched *WrestleMania* in a long time and I thought it was great. You know, I respect all those guys and I think I'd be proud and honored to work with any of those guys. I think they're doing a fantastic job and I know that these days it's very different from back in the '80s and '70s and '90s and all that. I think they're doing a fantastic job giving the people what they want, which is ultimately our goal. Whichever time period you want, that's the name of the game — going in there and giving the fans what they pay for, which is entertainment and thrills and for them to be coming out of that arena or watching the pay-per-view and going, "Wow, that's fantastic." It's like that *WrestleMania* . . . I was with a couple of friends here and we went to see it. They were so in awe of wrestling and realized that these guys put their lives on the line doing so many moves that are dangerous. . . . And I also was privileged to see that match — Flair against Shawn Michaels — two guys I wrestled many, many times. Ric Flair is another guy . . . I have so much respect for him because I had so many matches against him in Japan when he was NWA World Champion and I was AWA. I always respected him, in and out of the ring, and for him to retire this way, I thought it was perfect. So, you know, I can't pinpoint just the one guy, but I'd be honored with any of those guys.

Ahmed Johnson: Man, that's a question. Can I name two people? Mad Dog Buzz Sawyer and Nikita Koloff. [Nikita] was one of my idols growing up.

Bushwhacker Luke Williams: Well, I'm gonna tell you straight away, I'm a tag team man. On my toes and my hands, I can count the number of single matches I've had in the last 20 years, and I'm telling you the truth there. A tag team I looked at for years, and they were villains too — I'm going back many years now — it's Ray Stevens and Pat Patterson. They were one of the greatest tag teams I saw of all time. . . . Their best run was on the West Coast; you're from the East Coast. But Frisco, L.A — West Coast. They were a team, and I seen tapes of them, I said, "This is one hell of a team. I wish I was in the ring." I've been in the ring with some [great] teams too, mate. Ricky Steamboat and the Indian, Jay Youngblood. They were one hell of a team in the Carolinas when I first came there in '80, '81. We were wrestling them throughout the Carolinas. They were one hell of a team too, mate . . . these guys were masters.

Terry Funk: Well . . . I damn near wrestled them all. You know what? It's again, my gosh . . . What a difficult question for me, because right now there's so many guys that I did wrestle that would be excluded. But, a couple of guys . . . This might sound funny to you, but maybe the real Gorgeous George, George Wagner. I would have had a good payday, that's for sure. Maybe a Rikidozan, from Japan, when he was in his heyday and it was just chaos over there. I was in the ring with Don Leo [Jonathan] — I always wanted to be. Whenever I could be in the ring with Don Leo, I was in the ring with him. Was in the ring with Lou Thesz. Was in the ring with Pat O'Connor. Was in the ring with Bob Geigel. And on and on and on and on and on and on. Iron Mike DiBiase. If I could [pick] somebody I'd like to wrestle again, probably Iron Mike. If I could have a team partner, you know who that would be? That I had once before, and I'd love to have again, I'd love to be with my father one more night. Those were wonderful days and wonderful people. I'll tell you the guy I would have loved to be in the ring with and never was: that is Eddie Graham, one of the truly best minds, if not the best mind, in the wrestling business ever, and one of the truly great, great workers . . . it would be Eddie, probably, more than anyone else I can think of at this time.

Pat "Simon Diamond" Kenney: I would have liked to have wrestled Flair. I would have liked to have wrestled Tully [Blanchard]. You know, another guy I would have loved to wrestle was Kurt [Angle]. I sit there and I watch him. . . . Man, this guy is taking people's heads off. He's moving a thousand miles an hour. I look at him and just wonder if I could keep up with him. That's more of just a pride thing. But, I mean, Kurt's legit. People talk about how this guy's a tough guy. This guy's a shooter. This guy's a bad ass. This guy's this, this guy's that. The bottom line is the guy's an Olympic gold medalist — number one. Number two: he's a phenomenal pro wrestler. You know another guy I'd like to wrestle is Joe, Samoa Joe. Because his style's so different. When he first came into TNA and was seen nationally for the first time, it was like, wow.

Greg Valentine: Well, I used to say Chris Benoit . . . because I liked his style. I worked with him one time in WCW and I believe that's on one of his tapes or DVDs. That particular match, I really enjoyed. But there's such a horrible stigma about Chris Benoit now, I really can't say that anymore. I guess, I don't know out of the current guys wrestling. Because I wrestled Shawn Michaels; obviously, he's still out there. I guess maybe the Rock. We would have done well together. Or against Randy Orton as a babyface — that would have been good.

Jesse Ventura: I pick Superstar Billy Graham, because I think it would have been like the two twins meeting. Billy was my inspiration to get in the ring. By the time I reached my pinnacle, naturally, Billy was on the twilight of his career — had changed his image, with the shaved head, and had all the health problems. But in his prime, I would have loved to see a tag team, in our primes, of Superstar Billy Graham and Jesse "The Body" Ventura.

Sean Mooney: From the wrestling world . . . that's a really good question. I think I really had the chance to work with the best of the best. You know, I wish I could have done more with Jesse [Ventura], because I was like the perfect foil for him. He used to call me the country club kid or something like that. He was just really good. He was so sharp in the stuff he would say. Who else? I wish I knew Andre younger. I got to be pretty good friends with him and he was . . . Talk about a misunderstood human. I think that all you have to do is see *Princess Bride* to really capture who that guy was. He was so great in that. You gotta imagine, he lived in a fishbowl his whole life. He would sit in airports and I remember it got to the point where he would not acknowledge anybody because it did him no good. People would come by with their kid, "Can we take a picture with you? Can we?" It was kind of sad that that's the way it had to be, but he was really a gentle soul. I think to have worked with him when he was in the ring — I think that would have been a hoot.

Jackie Gayda-Haas: Goodness gracious, I would probably have to say someone as electrifying to work off of as Hulk Hogan or the Rock. Even, really, Stone Cold. I've done a couple of things with him here and there. But when you've got such a . . . presence about you. Other than that, Miss Elizabeth would definitely be somebody . . . Even Sunny. I've ran into her several times too, but back in the day when it was something special to be a woman manager. To really learn that art and learn that aspect of the business and perfect that craft — that's something I think would really be cool.

Scott D'Amore: God, trying to pick one . . . There was talk of it happening at one point a few years back — [it] would probably be Hulk Hogan. Maybe it's a clichéd answer; maybe saying Hulk isn't the coolest thing. I mean, yeah, I would have loved to have been in the ring with Harley Race — you know, just because of how cool he is and how awesome he is. I got to be in the ring with Ric Flair. I got to be in the ring with Arn Anderson. I've been in the ring with the Rock. I've been in the ring with Steve Austin.

Arn Anderson is the one who blew my mind when I was in the ring with him — because he was Arn Anderson, he's the Enforcer! But there would be something about doing something with Hulk; because whether you like Hulk or whether you hate Hulk, Hulk is the biggest star this business has ever had. There can be an argument now made for the Rock, absolutely. But Hulk is a wrestling guy. Dwayne Johnson was a good guy. I traveled with him some. He was awesome. He was an amazing performer. Hell, he was probably a better in-ring performer than Hulk. But there is something special about Hulk Hogan. To this day, if you're in a room and Hulk Hogan walks into that room, he doesn't have to say a word. Nobody has to acknowledge anything. Every head in that room turns and looks at Hulk. Edge's wedding, a couple of years ago, Hulk showed up. I always joke with Edge that my wedding present to him was that I got Hulk to come to his wedding. Because I'm the one who told him it was right around the corner from Hulk's house. Edge never invited Hulk because he never thought Hulk Hogan would come to his wedding. I was with Jimmy Hart. Hulk called Jimmy. When I told Hulk I was going to be right by there for the wedding, he said he was going to show up and sure enough he did. When he walked into that room, my now-ex girlfriend turned around with this face. She was 24 at the time — all of a sudden, she turned six years old. She turned around, stopped the conversation, ripped me away from Chris Jericho, and she goes, "Hulk Hogan's here!" I go, "Yeah?" She goes, "He's real!" I was like, "Yeah . . ." She's like, "He's really here in this room!" That's the extreme . . . response, but it doesn't matter. Anywhere Hulk goes, people gravitate to him. And if Hulk hadn't been a wrestling star, he'd have been a star in something else because people gravitate to him. He just exudes cool. At 50 years old, he can walk around wearing a bandana and spandex pants with cowboy boots, a weight belt, and a sleeveless tuxedo shirt and nobody bats an eye!

Paul Ellering: I really enjoyed working . . . anytime Ric Flair was around. I liked being around Ric. Ric is a consummate . . . He's good in the ring; he's good out of the ring. He's fun to be around. As far as new guys, I can't even tell you, because I don't know who there is.

The Stro: Kurt Angle comes to mind, actually. You know, because Kurt, to me, is still pound-for-pound one of the best wrestling athletes out there. I mean the guy's phenomenal. I would have liked to have done the deal with Ricky Steamboat . . . I had the opportunity to train with him at one of the wrestling seminars for Elite Pro Wrestling Training that Les Thatcher promoted. Just to train with the guy was amazing because I met him years ago near Lake Norman outside of Charlotte. We happened to have dinner together. Watch his matches with Flair and the matches he had with the Briscos. I've always wanted to do some kind of deal with me and Ricky Steamboat, because I thought he had tremendous, tremendous talent.

Ivan Koloff: I've often wondered about some guys I never got to wrestle, like Karl Gotch. He was a tough guy and all that. I had the honor of wrestling Lou Thesz and Stu Hart and some of the old timers like that . . . I guess probably those names which would be impossible, of course, now, to have wrestled, because of the age difference. . . . Probably, see, I don't watch religiously and I'm not up on all the guys in there today. I don't know, out of respect for him, Shawn Michaels, I'd love to have wrestled because he's still out there today. Back in my heyday, a guy like Rey Mysterio, because I did wrestle Mil Mascaras and he reminds me a bit, although Rey does even more stuff than Mil Mascaras did — that'd be sort of a different kind of match. As far as the big guys are concerned — wow. At the right time, a guy like the Undertaker. You know, because I could mold him with his style. He's such a giant, but yet a great performer. You know, I think I could have had a good match with him . . . but there's so many. It's not fair to pick one out. I've been in there with Harley Race, The Funks, The Valiants, Road Warriors, so many of the names . . . Ray Stevens, Dick Murdoch. Man, even the old timers like Haystacks Calhoun, Gorilla Monsoon, some of the guys like that, Lou Thesz . . . I've wrestled guys like Andre the Giant and Bruno Sammartino — man, it's like you've done it all. Even though there's so many great athletes out there today, I'd like to have been able to have a wrestling program . . . with any of them.

Al Snow: Oh gosh, probably Ray Stevens or Dr. Jerry Graham Sr. — the original Sheik. These are all names I imagine most people wouldn't even know nowadays, but um . . . Jerry Lawler. God, he is without a doubt probably the greatest worker in the business ever. Honestly. The more I — the longer I've been in the business — the more appreciation I have grown to have for Lawler. I think Lawler's better, and people will argue with me about this I'm sure, and probably take offense to it. But I'll tell you this right now. I think Lawler is, without a doubt, the best worker ever in the business. I think he's better than Flair. I think he's better than anybody. I really do. It's one thing, you know, to go from territory to territory and get stuff over. A lot of people these days misunderstand a lot of stuff. Ole Anderson, too. As much as, personally, I used to dislike him because of how he and Gene [Anderson] treated me when I went down there to try out, the guy was an incredible worker and knew what he was doing to be able to go to a territory and stay there and continue to make money. Now keep in mind, a promoter's not going to keep you in a territory unless you made money. Now, Jerry Lawler was able to stay in Memphis for not just once in a while, but for years. They'd have that sellout of the Memphis Coliseum every Monday night for years, you know, and that's attributable to Lawler. And still, to this day, Vince, himself, if he needs to get someone over . . . You know, he needs to get them over, put them in a program to make them in some way — who does he put them in there with? Jerry Lawler. And Lawler's so great on the mic. Honestly, I never really, really realized it. When I was younger, same as a lot of people, "Oh well, it's Flair." And Ric Flair's an amazing worker, but Jerry Lawler, I have to say, is probably the best ever. I really think he is. I think he's underappreciated. I don't think people realize it. That's how good he is — that people don't realize how good he is.

Kid Kash: I would say most likely Dynamite Kid. . . . I was a wrestling fan growing up, but not a huge wrestling fan, you know? I spent most of my life, you know, my dad was a professional boxer. So I started boxing at seven years old. Then I started taking martial arts at, like, ten years old. So I watched wrestling, but I was more into, you know, the real stuff: contact fighting and stuff like that. But the first time I ever saw Dynamite Kid, it just blew me away. Because I've never seen a short guy with so much muscle, first of all. He's so damn aggressive, and up until that time, I hadn't seen anybody be real aggressive. I mean you could watch TV and if you paid close enough attention, even as a fan, you can tell where they messed up and stuff like that. You could see where a spot got blown and stuff like that. You could see where they pulled punches. They'd go for a super kick and miss by about a foot and someone would still bump for it. But I would see Dynamite Kid out there just beating the ever-living hell out of somebody, man. And I was like, "Damn! I like that guy!" Because of him, I started watching wrestling even more.

Bruno Sammartino: Number of guys . . . Dory Funk — or any of the Funks, because I think they were great. I like Dory and I like Terry Funk. I think those guys are great. I wish I would have had the opportunity. I was tag team partners with Terry in one match, one time, in Japan. But I wish I would have had the opportunity to wrestle both of those guys, because I believe, in my heart, we could have had great, great matches.

Zach Gowen: I would wrestle Umaga. I always enjoyed wrestling bigger guys. I think there's a hell of a story to tell there. As far as a big monster against a small underdog one-legged kid. You know what I mean? I think there's stuff there. We could have a good match in the ring and I think it would make sense. I think it would be really cool to work something like that. I saw Umaga vs. Spanky [Brian Kendrick] on *Raw* not too long ago and it was just unbelievable.

Dan Severn: I've always been referred to as a throwback to days gone by, so I would have fit in more to the era of Harley Races . . . the Dory Funks, Terry Funks, Brisco Brothers, and names of that nature.

With that being said, it would only be fitting that I would wrestle a match against the man on top — and that is Lou Thesz.

Mae Young: I tell you what — I have, on my 100th birthday, an appointment to wrestle Stephanie McMahon's daughter, Aurora Rose. And that's gonna be my opponent on my 100th birthday. Stephanie has already promised me that I can do that, so I'm gonna do that. I'll be there. . . .

Ron "The Truth" Killings: Ah man, probably the Rock. Probably the Rock or Austin . . . between him and Stone Cold.

Jazz: A girl that never even got the opportunity to be in WWE. And that's Miss Passion. Her and I worked together on the indies one time. When we get out in the ring, the boys hate to follow us. We tear the house down, bro. Her name is Amy and she was in OVW. I don't know why she didn't get the opportunity to go up. She most definitely had the ability and the skills . . . and she worked with a lot of those girls who are up there now. The Mickie Jameses and Beth Phoenixes and Jillian Halls. She worked with all those girls, and her style is very, very similar to mine. I broke her in, but we finished her up.

Jimmy Valiant: My goodness, brother, man . . . I don't know . . . 10,000 matches. People say, "Who was your best, favorite match?" I have no idea. Man, I've wrestled all the champs, from Lou Thesz, you know, all the way up. Man, I changed the Rock's diapers, you know, brother. Hey, James, I really did smell what the Rock was cooking. . . . In 1980, I was in Memphis and me and his father was tag team champion — Rocky Johnson. And we were around all these kids, all these stars. Second generation, third generation. I wrestled [Randy] Orton's father, you know, of course, Bob Orton Jr., but I wrestled with Bob Orton Jr.'s father, you know, "The Big O," Bob Orton Sr. . . . My goodness, I have no idea, brother. Dick the Bruiser. I loved to wrestle that cat, you know. I wrestled him 1,000 times. Jerry "The King" Lawler, man. These were probably two of my favorites. Ivan Koloff, man — I had a nine-month run with him. Seven days a week, I wrestled Ivan for nine months. Just terrific, terrific talent.

Fred "Tugboat/Typhoon/Shockmaster" Ottman: Oh my God, I can't. I had the opportunity to work with so many great people. I mean, God . . . Guys I grew up on, I mean, down here in Florida it was like having a mini-WWF on all the time, as far as Florida Championship Wrestling is concerned. Everybody wanted to come down to Florida because the weather's great and the trips are short. So you go to the beach and work at night — so a lot of people came down to Florida to work. God, I don't know — I admired guys like Ernie "The Cat" Ladd. Jake the Snake's dad, Grizzly Smith. I worked in Texas when they'd bring down One Man Gang to work with me all the time. The greatest inspiration I think I had in the early part of my years was working in Texas and meeting all those guys. The Von Erichs were all really nice guys. I learned a lot from them. I mean, Kerry Von Erich was on the road with me a week — the whole week or ten days — prior to him going home, and that's when he died. When he went home. He was just such an awesome guy. I don't know if you remember Frank Goodish, Bruiser Brody. One of the biggest inspirations of my life was having the opportunity to be around him and listen. He was just a legend in Japan. Just unbelievable, the power he had. He was a machine in the ring. If I could have ever worked like somebody, it would be that man there. You know what, he was tremendous. He'd always tell me, "Let me tell you something, kid . . ." He'd watch the matches and that, and he's quiet. His whole life revolved around his son and his wife. I mean, you know, he says, "They come to watch the big men. . . . They come to see us, and when you go out there, take care of yourself, kid." There's a lot of guys . . . and their characters were larger than they were in the ring.

Wrestling Society X owner Kevin Kleinrock: It would have been nice to have a major, major name to be able to kind of bring in that audience [to Wrestling Society X]. One person who wasn't in WWE or TNA at the time that I wanted to bring onto the show was Terry Funk. We had used Terry back in XPW, and Terry and I had come in contact. He was actually the first person to come out and say that he was so excited that we were going to do a half-hour show, because no one had done that before and it would be a great way to keep the action fast-paced and keep the audience's attention. Then schedule-wise, we weren't able to work things out to bring him in. And then, in terms of was there a worker out there that we would have wanted to bring in . . . I have to be honest . . . For the most part, even looking at the WWE and TNA rosters, there weren't many people that would have fit into what we were doing. I think Edge definitely would have been a good guy to have. I've been a fan both of his workrate and his personality and his character for a long time. But really, looking at the WWE roster at the time, he was probably one of the very few people I would have thought we could bring in. Then from the TNA side, I think Samoa Joe would have been a great addition to our roster. I think I was at Joe's first match ever in southern California. I'm very familiar with his career and [the] progression of his career. I think his style would have worked in well with what we were trying to do.

"Masterpiece" Chris Masters: Who would I wrestle in their prime and why? I mean, there's a lot of people, for a lot of different reasons, in terms of getting in the ring with. But I think anybody . . . one of the most typical answers and you've probably heard this before, would be: the Hulkster. I never got to get in the ring with the Hulkster and just feel the energy when Hulk Hogan comes out — because that's a different energy. Hulk Hogan established himself and built a name. He is immortal. He really is "The Immortal Hulk Hogan," and we still see him, and he still generates that response and reaction. It's like that's never gonna go away. I mean, it seems like he really does have some form of immortality. Even . . . the Triple Hs and Shawns [Michaels], they all went through a point where they obviously wanted to work Hulk Hogan, and they all got to do it. If you're asking me, I'd definitely love to go out there and be in the ring with Hulk Hogan and feel that energy.

Aaron "The Idol" Stevens: I have to say Owen Hart. I just think Owen was so good, and it was like the more I got involved in the actual wrestling business, and the more I understood about psychology and how to control a crowd, the better and better Owen Hart got . . . you know, through my eyes. He's just somebody I would have loved to get in there with.

Rodney Mack: As far as being a fan, I would always have loved to wrestle Ric Flair. That's always a dream match and from WWE, in my time, I think that, you know, we cheated the fans out of a Goldberg match. I think that Goldberg and I could have had a great match.

Ernest "The Cat" Miller: It's two of them, man. Ernie "The Cat" Ladd and Abdullah the Butcher. I was watching on YouTube a couple of nights ago, I just happened to click on the old matches — man, they were so entertaining. They didn't do all that high-flying stuff. They didn't take the break-neck kind of bumps. It was a story they were telling. It was like watching a mini-movie, you know? It was just fun. I wish I could have worked with those guys.

Too Cold Scorpio: There's a couple I could name. To start, I'd probably say Shawn Michaels. I always thought that he was a chameleon. A guy who could change his style, kind of like me, to wrestle against anybody he fights with, no matter if he was smaller, bigger, or whatever. Bret Hart, I've always thought I could just have a great match with him because of his technical style of wrestling and his storytelling. There's always been Curt Hennig, a guy that could bump like he could bump and tell a story like he could tell. I always figured we could just burn down the house and be one of the greatest matches of all time. Another person, as well, as far as on the Japanese side, would be Muta. I would always like to fight Muta, on a one-on-one championship match instead of the short-style matches I've had with him.

ECW creator and PWU owner Tod Gordon: Wow . . . it's like *Inside the Actors Studio*, and the standard question at the end. Somebody I just wish I had the opportunity with? Umm . . . I think of Kurt Angle, who we almost started with, but I don't know that I would have known what he was capable of yet. Who knew how fast he'd grow into a role? There's like a handful of guys, like Hogan or the Rock or Sting, that didn't work for us at some point or another. So I can't really say. . . . There were the Steiners, like I said, Abdullah the Butcher, Stan Hansen, everybody came down to work it seemed like. I can't imagine anyone that I really have any regret of not having the opportunity to work with.

Shawn Daivari: Oh man, that's tough. Two names come to mind. One would be Mick Foley, because Mick is always able to draw that little extra something out of many a people. I've seen it so many times . . . Like, he'll have a whole bunch of matches with a whole bunch of people. Some are memorable, some aren't. But when he does have the memorable match, and he pulls that little extra something out of someone, it's unbelievable. It burns an image in your mind forever. I can remember moments like the match he had with Randy Orton . . . that was a specific match when he pulled a little extra something out of Randy Orton and, at that point in time, it was the best performance we had ever seen out of him. Same thing with Triple H, when Triple H was just getting started in '99, I believe. In that era, they had a match at the Royal Rumble where I think he pulled a little extra something out of Triple H . . . and it goes on and on with so many different people. He's super good at pulling that little extra something out of someone. Edge is another one. That match he had with Edge, I think, was one of Edge's greatest matches. . . .

The other one would obviously be Shawn Michaels. Now, I know people would say I wrestled him before, but there's a difference between a house show match, a TV match, a pay-per-view match, and a WrestleMania match. We've done the house show match. We've done the TV matches. But those are just everyday things for Shawn. When Shawn puts on his pay-per-view boots or even more specially, his WrestleMania boots, what he does, there's nobody in the world who can touch him. And that's something I'd love to get . . . one of those, with him. A pay-per-view match or even, better yet, a WrestleMania match, because when he comes to those, he puts everything out on the table and I've yet to see him under-deliver, even deliver, to expectations. He always delivers beyond expectations every single time.

Tammy "Sunny" Sytch: Oh my God, I don't know . . . I worked with, like, everybody. Oh, I always wanted to manage Ric Flair. From day one, I said I always want to be the Nature Girl — I want to manage Ric Flair. I thought that would have been awesome. Another person I always wanted to manage, and we actually were going to work together before he died, was Curt Hennig. Yeah, there were plans on making us, like, "the Perfect Couple." Not plans, but talk about it. Because Curt and I got along great and we, every time we had to do anything together, we clicked. He and I really, really worked well together, and there was talk about putting us together as manager and wrestler. Then he passed away, so that was the end of that. But yeah, those two I always wanted to do something with, and just never had a chance to.

Nick "Eugene" Dinsmore: That's a long list, man. . . . Without a doubt, Dynamite Kid would be on there. I always wanted to meet Owen Hart, and my first day with WWE, doing an extra, was unfortunately the day after Owen passed away. I never had a match with Rey Mysterio when I was younger and a bit more agile — I always wanted to wrestle him. So, Rey Mysterio . . .

Damien Demento: Well, when I was with the WWE, somebody I wanted to talk a match out with, who was actually an artist himself, was Bret Hart — the champ, right? We got along well and so, if we're in a quiet restaurant or something and not too many people around, because back then it was still heels and babies, I'd sit down and have lunch or dinner with him, and he was a real nice guy. He wasn't like he just stayed around with the upper crust of wrestlers. He hung out with everybody, even a little guy like Damien Demento. And then we both had in common that we would draw and stuff. I said that if I ever had a match with him, I'd like to do something that's kind of interesting because everyone's smart to the business. The spot I mentioned to him was that we'd start off just with the regular match, you know? Regular, eh? A clothesline — ba, ba, ba — throw the guy into the turnbuckle, and then, you know, go back and forth a little bit. Ordinary spots. Then I said, "But what if we threw something in there where it looked like a mess-up?" Where, obviously, one of us called the spot, but the other guy messed it up? We both hit the ropes. We come towards each other and the both of us duck. So somebody called duck, right? Duck elbow. Duck clothesline. And then there was gonna be a spot after that . . . but we both duck and we run into each other with our heads down and it looks like a complete and utter blunder. And all the marks are gonna say, "Uh, looks like somebody messed up the spot." And, at that point, one of us gets up — really, really upset — and starts laying it into the other guy, looking like it's turning into a real fight because somebody messed up a spot. I thought that would have been pretty cool. Bret thought about it for a while and he was like, "I don't know." 'Cause it does sound like a mess-up, and him, being the consummate pro, he doesn't make mistakes. He's the guy who's the best there ever was and the best there ever will be. But I thought that would have been an interesting way to open up a match. Making it look like it's an ordinary match, but a legitimate mess-up, and one of the guys gets pissed off and just starts laying into — with potatoes — into the other guy. So that's where my mind was at — I guess I was from the outer reaches of your mind.

Juvi Guerrera: I don't know but . . . maybe like I have to say Tiger Mask. I have to say [Jushin] Liger. I have to say Great Muta influenced me a lot. The timing and the moves. Ric Flair — the way he ducks, you know? Scott Hall, you know? Those are the main guys, I guess. . . . Eddie [Guerrero]! Of course, Eddie. I think I'm, you know, of course it's Eddie and [Chris] Benoit. They were the two guys because, you know, Chris was very . . . intense, which I kind of liked. I would try to pick up something from him combined with Eddie. Because Eddie was like, more, more, spectacular. So I got really a lot from them. Those are the guys that inspired me a lot.

The One Man Gang: I don't know; I pretty much wrestled everybody that was around at that particular time. Shoot, that's hard to say for me . . . somebody today . . . that's Undertaker. I would like to have the One Man Gang go against the Undertaker.

Sylvain Grenier: That's a good question because I was lucky enough to be in the ring with Hogan, Flair, Rock. . . . But that's a really good question. I've been very fortunate so far with the people I've worked with. But I think, maybe because I worked with him and I know him, I think maybe an angle with Rock at his time would have been phenomenal. For me, as a personal level, because he can talk and . . . at the time I didn't think I could express myself so good. But now I can and I would love to go, uh, word fight with him.

Bill DeMott: Wow . . . I've had some great opportunities. I've been in the ring with some great people. If I had the opportunity to work with someone, you know what? I'll probably shock a lot of people by saying this, including myself, I've been in the ring with a lot — I mean Hall of Famers — like I said, I've had a lot of opportunities. I have never ever been in the ring with Triple H. Never. To my recollection, not even in any instance, at least physically. And I always felt like if I was in the ring with a certain star or person, they would know more about me or get a better feel for me, you know what I mean? It's one of those things . . . I wouldn't want to be in the ring with him because he is Triple H and because he is the Game. I like his thought process, and I know who trained him in Jody Hamilton and [Killer] Kowalski and stuff like that. . . . And I think I know what he's about because I've talked to him many, many times. I think it would have been very interesting to be in the ring with Triple H. I think it could have been something. A pretty good little setup there. But there's so many great guys out there, and I've been in the ring with so many. I mean, even going back, I've been in the ring with Harley Race and all those guys. I mean Flair and everybody. But I think it would have been interesting to see Bill DeMott and Triple H in there.

David Young: As far as tag teams go, I think I woulda loved, *loved*, to have got the chance to wrestle the Rockers. . . . I'm friends with Marty — I know Marty very well. But I still never wrestled him, and I would give anything just to, you know, be able to step in the ring with him or Shawn. Either one, that would be just so much fun. The thing about those guys, they were doing things then, that people today would look at and think, you know, that is something that everybody does. . . . But back then those guys were the ones who opened the door for, you know, the cruiserweights that you see today. I mean, Shawn and Marty, to me, in their day, were the best tag team in the world, and nobody could hold a candle to them. Period.

Dory Funk Jr.: I'd certainly like to have had a chance to wrestle Triple H. Oh yeah . . . I've always had a lot of respect for him.

Tito Santana: Well, besides Greg Valentine . . . And, from what I understand, Mr. Wonderful [Paul Orndorff] and I were supposed to have had an angle before Greg Valentine. I had some great matches with Mr. Wonderful, and I believe our styles complimented each other even more than me and Greg Valentine, you know? They had completely different styles. We had a match in St. Louis that Vince McMahon just couldn't believe. And he told us after the match was over that he couldn't believe the things we were doing in the ring, and it just clicked. Mr. Wonderful was a great heel, and I remember wrestling against him in L.A. — the place was packed. And a fan jumped up on his back and started punching him, you know? There had to be some pretty serious heat. . . . You don't see that too often, where a fan jumps up and starts beating up a heel. If I would have done an angle with Mr. Wonderful, I think it would have been very successful. I think the reason we didn't do it is because Mr. Wonderful was very temperamental, and I think Vince McMahon was afraid of him.

Jon Heidenreich: Gosh dog, man, somebody I'd like to work? I mean, I'd like to work Shawn Michaels, you know? He worked so many big guys. So many good . . . I mean, there's a ton more. Ric Flair. There's so many guys . . . I mean Shawn, man. He had so many matches with big guys, and I'm not gonna say he made them look awesome, but he had some great matches with them. He'd be nice to work, and say I've worked Shawn Michaels, you know? He's been over for a long time and still is. . . . Heck, Flair, Triple H, even [Randy] Orton. There's so many good — Kurt Angle. There's so many good guys up there that are so tremendous. I will say this — I got to get in the ring with Eddie Guerrero in a match that was one of the dark, dark matches, which is after TV. I got to work in a tag, I think it was. But just to get in the ring with him was amazing because I think the world of him as a wrestler and as a person, because he was somebody who was there for me when I went through a lot of rough times in my life with the hurricane [Katrina] and everything. I just thank God that I got to be in there with him. He's such a wonderful person and a beautiful person. It's just so sad we had to lose him. . . .

"Psycho" Sid Vicious: Let's see . . . Well, that's really easy. I would have enjoyed working with someone like Harley Race. I would have liked for it to be an extended angle, where I could learn. In my opinion, Harley Race is one of the greatest, smoothest workers of all time. He just went effortlessly through all his motions. I got a chance, a first-hand example, to see this. It was me, Ric Flair, Arn Anderson, and maybe Barry [Windham] against El Gigante, JYD, Sting, and [Lex] Luger in an eight-man. I've seen Harley Race make JYD look like a million bucks and that's hard to do. He was just so damn good. If I could have been that smooth, at my size, that would have just given me an extra — you know. And that's credibility. The word that comes along with Harley Race is credibility, and that's what I've tried to do in my career. Find people I see that have credibility and implement something from their career into mine. I've got a lot of weird characters in my character, but they all have credibility. One's like John Wayne. One's like Hannibal Lecter . . . outside wrestling characters. But my wrestling characters were the people who were a big influence on me were people like Ole Anderson, Pat Patterson. People like that, where I could ask a question and they automatically give me an answer, and I knew that was an answer I could keep the rest of my life. 'Cause they were just that good and that clear about things. And Vince [McMahon], as well. But I didn't get a chance to talk to Vince a lot about things like that because he was so busy. But whenever I had a chance to, he could also do the same thing.

Rob Conway: I would love to face, wrestle, or even meet the Macho Man Randy Savage. I never even met him. He was outside the WWE by the time I got there, so I never even met him. I loved to watch him. I loved his whole persona, and then the more and more I hear about how he's not really a stretch from how he really is . . . It just makes me want to meet him and wish I could have wrestled him even more.

Doug Basham: Bret Hart . . . I would have loved to work with Shawn Michaels as well, because he's one of the best in our biz. And I never got to get in the ring with Triple H either. That would have been quite an experience as well.

"Goldust" Dustin Rhodes (on wanting to work an angle with his father and brother): Hopefully the three of us can six-man tag. But me and my brother are trying to talk Dad into a — when Cody actually starts — having him do kind of the Goldberg deal, where he's winning and winning and he's undefeated. . . . So Goldust steps back in the picture and they know I'm his brother. So I start winning and winning and winning and winning. Finally I lose one, and Cody's still winning, and I go out there during Cody's match or something and keep him from winning. But now it's all just a big ploy. It's an act. The people are thinking I'm pissed off at my brother, and Dad comes out like, "Hey, wait a minute. What the hell are you doing, Dustin? You had your time in the ring, this and that, you know? Don't come out here and pull this shit like that." And then Cody comes around behind. We just lay into Dad and beat the holy crap out of him into a family deal. And Dad won't do it. He don't want to do it. But to have it work right, Vince [McMahon] comes out, "Hey, hey, hey, hey! This is my building. This is my show. I ain't gonna have no family squabbles" and shit. Then that could end up being a Vince and Dusty versus Dustin and Cody, you know? Or Vince and Dad and Hunter versus me, Cody, and, uh, whoever, you know?

Road Warrior Animal: I tell you what, I'll put a little different twist on that for you. One thing that I wish the wrestling business would have done — and they had a chance to do, and they never did it — is to have a six-man with the Road Warriors, LOD, and Hulk Hogan as one team. You would have done that and — we tried to get them to do that and reintroduce the six-man World Championship belts — I think it would have been a different kind of a gimmick and look. We could have run around the world doing that gimmick together with Hulk. It never happened. We were probably the only top guys to never team with Hulk. Only fought against him once, and I just think, for the business, that would have been such a great tool, for toys, vitamins, all marketing aspects, for the company to make money. People would have bought that and said, "Wow, Hulk Hogan and the Road Warriors against the Nation of Domination," or, you know, DX. It would have been the equalizer, and that's what our gimmick was always good at . . . being the equalizer. Hulk was always getting jumped by Bossman or Nailz or somebody else. But with this thing, if he would have kept getting jumped by Bossman, or he's getting jumped by somebody else, they say, "Who you gonna get, Hogan? Who you gonna get?" He goes, "I'll get somebody." All of a sudden [Hawk's opening growl before "What a Rush"] . . . The people would go crazy. That's what I think is one of the greatest things the fans got cheated out of, was seeing Hulk Hogan and the Road Warriors together on the same side fighting somebody. We would have painted him up yellow and red. Oh yeah, brother, I'm telling you. It would have worked because Hulk would have been the consummate professional. We were professional. We wanted to do it, but for some reason, they wouldn't go for it.

The former "A-Train" Giant Bernard: Oh man, there's so many of them. That's a tough question. You know, I'd love to work Vader in his prime. Or [Stan] Hansen in his prime . . . Big Bossman. I always had fun working with ol' Rey Mysterio, 'cause that's a fun match. Hogan would be cool. There's just so many of them, and I don't think I have one particular dream match. Vader, there was a guy who was six-foot-four, 300-plus plus, and he was agile. He could just move in the ring. He could do a moonsault . . . that was just beautiful. In his prime, he could go.

Paul Bearer (on who is the future of the industry): Man, I don't know. I truthfully don't know. It's not like I'm trying to avoid the question because I'm not. Because when Steve Austin started, I told you, I was his first manager when he started in the business. . . . He started at Chris Adams' Wrestling School at the Sportatorium in Dallas, and I was helping Chris run the school. I helped teach interviews and stuff. Steve was a part of that class. I remember, and I'm certainly not trying to take credit for anything Steve Austin has done because he had "it," whatever that might be. An intangible *it* — he had it. So there wasn't really a lot I could teach him. He was just a natural. For a while, when [Undertaker] was doing the American Bad Ass thing, I was working backstage at the Gorilla Position with Jerry Brisco, doing talent scout stuff. That's when Les Thatcher had the Heartland group. The OVW, of course, was still running. Rick Bassman had the Ultimate Wrestling in L.A. We had like four — and then Savio Vega was doing a little thing in

Puerto Rico, too. We had like — and then there was Memphis Championship Wrestling, too — we had like four or five farm clubs during that time, and I was going around to those different farm clubs and scouting talent. I was really having a blast just going from one to the other. I'd spend a few days in each one every week. A lot of those guys are on the roster today. John Cena's one of them. I scouted John Cena out in Ultimate when he was doing the Prototype for Rick Bassman. . . . Then [Randy] Orton — he was in OVW then. A lot of these guys were just starting during the time that I was doing the scouting stuff. So it's really hard for me to pick somebody. Like, I was going to say before I got off on that tangent . . . I would have never said that Steve Austin would turn out to be what it turned out to be. I knew he had it. I knew he'd be a success on some level. But what that level would be, I don't know. I wish I did have some sort of crystal ball to see the future of wrestling. But sometimes it gets very, very murky. You have to dust it off, as it comes to wrestling, to see any kind of future, because you don't know — it changes daily.

Jerry "The King" Lawler: You know what? That's one of the things about having a career as long as I've had. It will probably shock people when they hear about some of the people I have actually had the opportunity to wrestle. I mean, I started at a time when, early on in my career, very early on in my career, some of the biggest names in the history of wrestling were just finishing their careers — and I got to wrestle against those guys. Then, throughout my 30-year career, I've got to wrestle against just about everybody else. There aren't many guys I haven't been in the ring with. I go all the way back to having matches against guys like Lou Thesz. I had matches against guys like Wilbur Snyder, Dick the Bruiser, Bobo Brazil, the original Sheik. Then, moving up to guys like the Iron Sheik and Hulk Hogan. And then, moving up to guys like "Stone Cold" Steve Austin and the Rock. Then John Cena. Then the Undertaker. So, you know, when you look at it, I don't know if there's too many guys around who've had that career where they got to wrestle so many huge names from so many different eras. I mean, I probably spanned four, maybe four generations of the biggest stars in this industry. I don't know how many guys that are wrestling today can say they had a match with

Lou Thesz. Then, by the same token, can say that they had a match with Lou Thesz and John Cena.

Larry Zbyszko: You know, I guess Hogan would have been the guy in terms of making money. Because in the '80s, I'm in my prime, he's in his prime, he's the guy to make the money with. I think me and Magnum [Terry Allen] almost happened, where me and Magnum were gonna have some good shit down in the Carolinas in the early '80s . . . but then poor Terry got in that wreck.

Sylvester Terkay: Obviously, being from Pittsburgh, a hometown favorite type of — Bruno Sammartino would have been pretty interesting. That was like my mother's favorite wrestler. He made a lot of money. He was very physical. A very strong guy . . . And so, I'm a little bit more of a throwback. I like those older, rougher guys that want to go out there and, you know, have a slobberknocker, so to speak . . . to use the words of an announcer in WWE. To go out there and just be rough and physical and that type of thing . . . So I'm just more akin to that generation. The guys like Bruno Sammartino or even like a Stan Hansen. The guys like the Harley Races, and that era of guys, but I think Bruno Sammartino would have been good. If I could go back in time and jump him in the alley and beat him up, go have ourselves a pretty good match. I think it could have been a great sellout in something like a Madison Square Garden, you know? That's what I dream of. Of having that opportunity to step in the ring and have a good match with, say, like an Undertaker, or something. But in terms of some real good money, someone that was loved and was respected, was a good scientific wrestler but has a good balance of being physical also, I think Bruno would have been my pick.

"Dr. Death" Steve Williams: I really wished I would have worked against two guys, two of the major guys, man. That's Hulk Hogan and Stone Cold. I really feel like I could have been the greatest heel in the world to work against Terry, uh, Hulk Hogan, and against Stone Cold. We would have had a great run. I wished I would have got a chance. I really like Terry, Hulk Hogan. I've done a few things with him; he's a first class guy. Just like Stone Cold, man. I really know that, in my mind, and in my prime, we could have had great angles and had a great run. It would have went on for years, man. Because if you think back to my day, who was a great heel? Who was a guy that got the most heat? And you know what? First guy . . . tough guy . . . they'd think about Dr. Death Steve Williams.

Harley Race (about the future of the industry): I sent one up there, out of here, that I think, if they let this kid open up a little bit more, and they put him with another young guy — Trevor Murdoch is the kid that I'm referring to. Lance Cade is his partner. Lance has been around up there for several years and was stuck in a no-go position. But by having one kid come in, that kid takes that next step and was able to carry the other kid on up with him. Now how far will they allow that to go? Who knows? But the talent is there to go as high as they want . . .

"Shooter" Brent Albright: You know, on a physical level, I would love to wrestle Kurt Angle. I would love to see if I could hang with Kurt Angle. That guy's intensity, to me, he's just a different kind of wrestler. Maybe that's just me being worked by the business, but when I see Kurt Angle, he is just a different kind of wrestler. And I would love to see if I could hang with Kurt Angle. That to me would be great. Of course, there's a lot of other guys I would like to work. I'd love to have the opportunity to work Ric Flair. Love to have the opportunity to work, back in the day, a healthy Arn Anderson. Or a healthy Dean Malenko. Guys who are known for wrestling, and being intense, and having good matches.

Diamond Dallas Page: The Rock. I blew it. . . . When I came to WWF, he was filming *Scorpion King*. When I came back, they gave me the stalker gimmick. I'm thinking, bro, they know what they're doing . . . I don't have to do my own thinking here. They're gonna make this great . . . I didn't think past it. I said, "Well, I got this other idea. What about this People's Champion vs. People's Champion idea?" They shot it down, because, first of all, it wasn't their idea. Second, because they wanted to do the stalker thing. They already had Booker [T] set for the Rock. Looking back at it, they half-assed it. Because how do you stalk the toughest guy in the federation's wife when he's the toughest guy? . . . I don't think they were trying to demolish me the way people perceive it to be. I know because they offered Stone Cold the angle first. They sure as hell didn't want to demolish him.

Kevin Nash: Geez . . . I mean, if you had a career like most of us, I've been around for so long that I've wrestled, from this era. I've wrestled Rock and Steve [Austin]. I've wrestled Sting. I've wrestled Luger. I've wrestled Piper. I've wrestled Flair. I've wrestled Funk. The only guy — I mean Andre would be the only guy I'd think of. I mean Andre the Giant is the only guy I'd . . . Of course, I'd like to have wrestled Jesse [Ventura]. I'd love to be a babyface against him. I don't think I ever had a one-on-one with Tom Zenk. I'd love to wrestle Tom Zenk; I throw him into every interview now. That's my new thing. I keep throwing him out on my interviews and my stuff with TNA just to see if I can get him to respond. I always thought Tom was a good man. I'm hoping he'll resurface. Where you at, Z-Man? Where are you, Z-Man? Scott Hall wants to know too. We had the conversation two nights ago. Where the hell is Z-Man?

Rick Steiner: Hmm . . . That's, um, I mean, I was real fortunate. . . . When I was in the business, you know, I'd watch WWE and there's Macho Man and there's Hogan. In, more . . . the heyday I was in, there were Goldberg and there were Stings. So I was real fortunate to wrestle all those guys. Some of the younger guys? Um, you know, I even got a chance, when I first started, to work with the Samoans. The original, Afa and Sika. So, I mean, I always, when I was in Michigan, I always listened to Dick the Bruiser on the radio. It would be something to meet him. Then there's George "The Animal" Steele. He was from Michigan, a schoolteacher. So I got to meet a lot of those guys, but I don't know. I just made the most of the guys I worked with. It would have been fun to work with the Hart Foundation. That would have been a good one, as a tag team. I kind of look at everything as a tag team. I got to work with the Road Warriors. I got to work with the all best there was. The Briscos, they would have been fun to work with, because they're amateur guys. For the most part, I was content in what I did, and I got to work with the best in the business.

Bad News Brown: The guy that I wished I could have worked with, in the WWF, and if they let us work the way we worked up here, because I worked with Dynamite Kid up here. I always say that pound for pound he was the best there is. You still see these young guys today trying to emulate him. The guy was the best, and if we could have worked, he was on the downslide in the WWF with the British Bulldogs because he had so many injuries and everything. But if we could have worked a program there that Stu [Hart] let us work up here . . . I mean, we would have just made a whole bunch of money, you know? Because everything we did would look believable. People believed what we were doing, and it just was . . . we had some incredible matches. The arenas up here, when we hit the town, they'd actually have to turn people away because they couldn't get in. 'Cause they believed what they saw, and they actually wanted to see him kick my butt.

"The Doctor of Style" Slick: Well, there's several, but one that came to mind right away would have been King Kong Brody. Bruiser Brody. As a matter of fact, Bruiser Brody and I, had, um, probably, were going to New York if I hadn't gone with the Natural Butch Reed. And I think I would have liked working with the Freebirds in their heyday. They had electricity also, you know?

"The Mountie" Jacques Rougeau: To be honest with you, I'm very humbly saying, I've worked with everybody. . . . I've worked with Macho Man. I've worked with Jake the Snake. I've worked with Ricky Steamboat. I've worked with Hulk. I've worked with just about everybody. I guess one guy I wished I would have worked with would be the Rock. Because of his popularity . . . it would have been him. Apart from that, I've wrestled just about everybody in the business. The Undertaker, I've wrestled him one on one and had a great match with him. Sid Vicious. I remember them always using my character, the Mountie, to turn a heel babyface. You know, I remember Sid Vicious being the biggest heel in the business, and they needed to turn him babyface, and who'd they use? They used the Mountie. Because the Mountie would go in the ring and say, "You know what? I challenge any wrestler backstage and nobody can get the Mountie, because the Mountie always gets his man!" And then here came Sid Vicious. He was a top heel; everybody hated him. But when they knew he was gonna come kick my butt, he became a big hero. So I would have say the Rock, as the guy I never wrestled one on one with, but would have liked. . . .

"The Million Dollar Man" Ted DiBiase: I think I got to wrestle just about everybody that I wanted to during my active career. Since I've retired from the ring, out of today's talent, I don't think I ever got to wrestle Triple H. I never got to wrestle Hunter. I would have loved to wrestle Shawn Michaels today. You know, I wrestled Shawn when he was young and green. I had matches with him, but never big matches. Maybe a couple of tag team matches. I would love to work with Shawn today, with him being the talent that he's become. I think that would be awesome. There are some guys I'd like to work with just because I think, by working with them . . . they're skilled . . . I could help them get better. John Cena. You know, John Cena is not a great wrestler, but he's a great personality. Well, you know, Hulk Hogan was not a great wrestler. Not a great technical wrestler. He'd just do his gimmick very, very well. Timing is everything in the wrestling business. Everything in the ring, and it's everything out of the ring. It's like getting a break in the wrestling business is timing, too.

"Corporal" Kirschner: Any of the top champions that were out there, and I was actually fortunate enough to work with quite a few of them. I never really got to wrestle Ric Flair. I got to wrestle with the Funk Brothers, Ricky Steamboat, Randy Savage, but I never had a single match with Ric Flair in his prime. I would have enjoyed that. One of my favorite matches that I remember was wrestling Harley Race in Kemper Arena. It was sold out in Kansas City there. I would say that was one of the highlights of my career. Back when he was the King. And we wrestled, I remember, for 23 minutes, and he made me look like gold. Told me, "Take it easy, kid." We were in Harley's house that night, and he made me look like a thousand bucks.

Skandar Akbar: There's several of them that fit that category. You know, to single out one would be very, very difficult for me. Yeah, I don't know who I would single out. There was a lot of great stars in those days. A lot of great stars and, uh . . . when you broke in the business, if you got a chance to work with them, that was a bonus.

Nidia: You know what? I'd love to work with John Cena because he's so goofy. And get us together, it's a lot of fun. We used to work together and have a blast. He made me want to be a bad guy. Like, bad guys have all the fun.

Ivory: A hard question. I guess I would say, well . . . I'll tell you what. It wasn't one match, but an era that I missed out on, and I just really wish I could have been a part of more . . . and that was when I was off doing one of the *Tough Enoughs*. And the girls division really started coming up, and it was, you know, Trish and Victoria and Lita and Molly Holly and Jazz. Those were the main players, and they were just going at it, and Fit Finlay was in the mix, you know, as our agent. They were having great house show matches. They were having great pay-per-view angles. I was just sitting there watching these guys from, you know, L.A. or wherever, I was like "Ugh!" I was really chomping at the bit. We had one match, a pay-per-view match, with all the girls, Jacqueline — everybody. We had one really fun match where it was the one time I remember everyone in that wrestling ring knew how to wrestle. Such a feeling of comfort and, you know? You talk to a male wrestler, they don't have [only] one instance they remember where everyone in the ring could wrestle. That's the plight of a woman in this business.

Bull Buchanan: I've always said Flair. But, in recent times, another one has popped up. I would have loved to wrestle [Bruiser] Brody. Love to be able to work with Brody. I've really become, I mean I've always been a fan of his . . . but I have really become more and more a fan of his in the last few years. Once I started trying to figure out what he figured out a long time ago, made me appreciate that he was really ahead of his time in his thinking. Last tour in Japan, I read his book . . . Larry Matysik and [Brody's] wife wrote it. It's really good insight on the way I think the wrestling business should be . . . and a really good insight on the way that, as a professional wrestler, I think, you should view this business. He was very a shrewd business man. He was also . . . his ring psychology was very, very smart. He realized a lot of things that young guys could benefit from today. It's just a shame that he's not still around. But yeah, man, Flair, of course. Never got the opportunity to work with him, of course he was in WCW all those years. Once he actually came to WWE, at the time I was off the road, and I got back on the road, just doing dark matches and stuff. So, you know, you don't really get a chance to work with a guy like that, but I'd really like to work with Flair. And in the last few years, I'd have to put Brody in there too.

Disco Inferno: I would have always liked to face the Rock, you know? Yeah, just because he's an entertaining character. He has a lot of charisma. He's very gimmicky out there. You know, it's funny because, I always do, on independent shows, today, I do the Village People's Elbow . . .

Beautiful Bobby Eaton: That's a hard question to answer there. I'd probably like to work with, maybe, Buddy Rogers. That's what you're talking about, right? Yeah . . . shoot. Really, that's a hard thing for me to answer, because I can name a bunch of them, you know? Kurt Angle, of course. I'd like to fight him. I love Chris Benoit style of wrestling, but I couldn't keep up. Like his matches, Kurt Angle's matches, Eddie Guerrero's, Dean Malenko's, you know . . .

Dr. Tom Prichard: There's not just one. It would definitely have to be . . . I never had the chance to wrestle Terry Funk. I wrestled Dory in a tag match, but it'd have to be Terry Funk, Johnny Valentine, and Wahoo McDaniel. Just because. Those would be my top three.

Orlando Jordan: Wow, man. Who would I pick? Oh, man . . . It's a number of people. Rick Rude. Yeah, man, he was awesome. Dusty Rhodes back in the day. Man, I tell you. Dusty Rhodes back in the day. Ric Flair. Arn Anderson. Man, Arn was one of my favorite agents . . . Arn was awesome.

Nikolai Volkoff: One of my favorite opponents was Bruno Sammartino. A couple of reasons. For one, I was very green, you know, very young. Very strong and everything else, and uh, when I first wrestled in Madison Square Garden, I was main event and that was the first time it was sold-out. It was me against Bruno. And uh, all the guys say, "Hey, you guys did it. You guys did it." And I didn't know what they were talking about. So when I find out, my God, second best house ever they had before that was Bruno and Ivan Koloff. . . .

Nora "Molly Holly" Greenwald: That's a good question. I have worked with so many people, it's crazy — because almost every great star I've worked with . . . either behind the scenes or in the ring. As far as everyone from Hogan, Flair, Sting, Macho Man, Kevin Nash, Scott Hall, Ricky Steamboat, Arn Anderson, Madusa — like all the main stars you see on TV — I have been so blessed to either have some coaching from them or worked in the ring with them. I can't think of anyone, offhand, that . . . and even on the indies now, I just recently met Honky Tonk Man who, as a kid, I despised. I just put on a show Saturday with X-Pac and Greg Valentine. And it's just . . . I feel really complete in my career in that I don't have any thoughts in the back of mind. I mean, I've even been able to wrestle Sherri Martel when I was in WCW. That was great. So I can't think of anyone offhand that I never had a chance to work with or meet, because really, in my eight or so years of wrestling, I've just been so blessed in meeting and knowing so many people.

"Super Hero in Training" Ro-Z: Probably the Masked Superstar, man. He was always my favorite growing up. And it's kind of weird to say when you've got a family of wrestlers. But aside from my family, he was one of my favorites. You know, I probably would have liked working my cousin, Yokozuna, too. He was just a great, big man. Psychology. This and that. I know I would have learned a whole hell of a lot working with Yokozuna. He carried that persona about him through every company he worked for. I watched. We shared a bedroom together when I was nine years old. My dad was teaching him. So I've watched his career very thoroughly through the years — it was definitely a pleasure watching him in that ring.

Earl Hebner (on the future of the industry): They've got a lot of young talent down there, and A.J. [Styles] is gonna be great. His partner . . . Christopher Daniels. They're great, and they're young kids, you know? And down the road, they're gonna be superstars.

The Missing Link: The Undertaker. He used to come in the ring and walk real slow. I did the same thing at first, following Johnny Valentine, Greg's dad. So we all copy off each other. There are a number of people in the WWE that I would have loved to have wrestled. Shawn Michaels has turned into — I don't know what kind of person he's turned into . . . He's supposed to be a Christian, and the things he's doing on the television certainly are not derivative of Christianity. But he's doing all these things and he's really talented in many, many ways. And a good wrestler. There are some there — there aren't a lot of them — that know how to take a crowd of people and perform a professional wrestling match and keep the people very interested for a half hour.

D-Lo Brown: The sentimental pick — I'd love to have a match with Ron Simmons. Just because that would be so cool, to be in there with him. The second one, I'd have to say, I'd love to have a match with Shawn Michaels. Never had a match with him. Would love to take the Superkick one time. You remember when DX first formed, he was there and he got hurt and they quickly replaced him — that's when they brought in Road Dogg and Billy. So we never got a chance to interact. I would love to go out there and wrestle Shawn. But the first thing, I'd definitely like to wrestle Ron Simmons.

Tracy Smothers: Vince McMahon could go to hell. I got friends dead and in their grave indirectly because of him. Because he cut out all the jobs. There used to be a lot more jobs in this business. I'm 43 years old. I work when I want. I'm staying busy. I'm having a blast. I'm having more fun at it. I don't have to, you know, I don't have to take their crap. But I would love to go fight any of [the WWE wrestlers involved in the first One Night Stand PPV]. It wouldn't have to be in the ring either. They don't like what I'm saying, I ain't hard to find. I'm not hard to find. And I'm not saying I can beat them up. It ain't got nothing to do with trying to get attention. A little bit, yes. Sure it does, a little bit. Sure, it helps. Six hours after I made that challenge to Kurt Angle, I got a three-month tour of Europe. So, you know, who's the dummy here?

Buff Bagwell: I really don't have one. I'm gonna be honest with you, because I just don't. I've wrestled so many guys, for so long, that, you know, I really don't have any regrets. So I just don't have that kind of answer for you. I answered every problem I had to do. I wrestled every person I wanted to wrestle. You know, my gimmick wasn't really wrestling. It was more, you know . . . entertainment. So I didn't really have, you know, that worker mentality of where "I wish I had a chance to work Al Snow because he's a great worker." My job was — I was a good worker, but at the same time, I was an entertainer more than a worker. So, um, I think I covered that and had a great time doing it. No regrets at all. I had a blast. There's not too many guys that I turn on the TV and say, "That guy's got it." But I do like the Masterlock guy [Chris Masters]. I like him. I think he's got a chance at doing something.

Brother D-Von: Hulk Hogan. I'm a big Hulk Hogan fan. A lot of interviews, when people ask me who I looked up to — I looked up to Hogan. I was a huge Hulkamaniac. I know Edge, when he was teaming up with him, me and Edge would always get in the argument saying that he was the biggest Hulkamaniac around. Me and Edge always argued with each other and disagreed. Hogan was someone that I had looked up to. I grew up in Brooklyn, New York. I was trying to rush home to see what Hogan was gonna do next. That was my biggest thing. I idolized the man. I feel my role model was him. It was a great feeling actually, when we were on *Smackdown* together, changing in the same locker room. He's the man I looked up to. It was no different than Triple H looking up to Ric Flair growing up in the business. Hulk Hogan looking up to Superstar Billy Graham, you know? Ric Flair looking up to Buddy Rogers, you know? And the thing about it is . . . when you grow up and finally make that dream come true . . . you're working side by side with . . . It's a great feeling.

The Iron Sheik: It is a great, excellent question you ask. . . . Good friend of mine, Mr. Kurt Angle. He's a great performer. Great shooter. Number one, eh, Olympic gold medal in the, eh, '96? As a matter fact, I watched his match. I drove to Georgia. He wrestled my countryman — Iranian. The score was two on two. But Mr., eh, Kurt Angle — he come gold medal, Olympic 1996. Atlanta, Georgia. He's a great, great, great shooter. That means college wrestler, gold medal — and also, he's a great performer and professional. Like I say, I'm 65 years old now. Mr. Kurt Angle is younger than me. As far as I know, he's a great performer. He's a great shooter. Olympic gold medal. The only wish I had was younger so I can wrestle with Mr. Kurt Angle from Pittsburgh, Pennsylv-on-nia. Great performer. Great shooter, and he remind me of Bruno Sammartino. Both of them from Pennsylv-on-ia, and both of them great shooter and great performer.

Koko B. Ware: I was there for the *[Raw* Homecoming] on USA. You know, when they brought all the legends back. I was very, very impressed at the generation they have now. They were so polite. Man, they were just so nice. I mean, I just had a great time with Triple H, Batista, even Ric Flair. He's part of my generation, but I'm talking about these new guys. Edge — and the young ladies. The whole, I mean . . . it was just like a warm welcome . . .

"The Fallen Angel"/Curry Man Christopher Daniels: I'd prob-ably have to say Ricky Steamboat. He's someone I was a big fan of. Not just as a wrestler, but before that, when I was a fan watching it. I was always a fan of his work. Even before I understood pro wrestling, as I do today as a wrestler, I was someone who appreciated his efforts and hard work. Once you learn what pro wrestling is about, and you look at his stuff, it takes on a whole new meaning. . . . So, I'd probably have to say Ricky Steamboat.

A.J. Styles: I would say not just one guy, but to go back to the era when it was [Jushin] Liger and Benoit and Eddie [Guerrero] and Dean Malenko, and those guys were coming up at the same time. You know, Fit Finlay was in there. Too Cold Scorpio. I would love to be in there with those guys. Chris Jericho was also in there. I would love to have come up with those guys and got to wrestle in front of those big ol' crowds. Not really in the States, but in Japan — for the Junior Heavyweight Title in New Japan. I think that would have been some of the best matches that I would have gotten. . . .

Christian Cage: Wrestling as a heel, I think I would love to go back and have a thirty to sixty minute match with Ricky Steamboat. It was cool [to know Ricky Steamboat in WWE as a trainer]. He would come up and we'd talk. . . . He'd tell me he was a fan of my work and he enjoyed watching me. That means a lot, when you hear guys like that say stuff like that.

Elix Skipper: Ooo . . . I can wrestle anyone I want to . . . it would be Great Muta back in his best day. Back when he used to wrestle Sting, and first came to WCW . . . Oh man, just watching him reminds me of the cruiserweight style, the X-Division style — where he was doing the crazy things and, you know, just watching things like that is the reason you have the X-Division now.

Rhino: I'd like to wrestle Hulk Hogan, late '80s. And the Honky Tonk Man, because I was just a mark for him.

Samoa Joe: I'd love to wrestle Jumbo Tsuruta. Especially right before his retirement — in his latter years, with All Japan, I thought he was really great. I always wanted to wrestle Tenryu, if he was around today.

Kamala: I can't think of . . . anybody. I just can't, because I think I wrestled about all of them. You know, like Andre — and I used to even watch Andre, you know before I started wrestling — and I end up wrestling a guy I had watched on television.

Vince Russo: [There's] a guy I'm real, real high on that hasn't really made his mark on the top level yet. A guy named Jimmy Rave, who I know works a lot of Ring of Honor, who I think is absolutely tremendous.

Aaron "Jesus" Aguilera: I have the utmost respect for Fallen Angel [Chris Daniels], but I've already wrestled him. So I would love to wrestle A.J. Styles. I would love to, man, because he's freakin' awesome. I mean, what can I say about A.J. that hasn't been said already? You know? I think the matchup with the lightweight-cruiserweight-big man thing might be pretty intriguing. And then I never got to wrestle my good friend Paul London. He's my friend out of the ring. He's my brother-in-Christ out of the ring. But in between the ropes, man — you know what I'm saying? If he wants to call out Jesus, we can do this. So I'd have to say in WWE, it would be Paul London. In TNA, it would be A.J. Styles.

Matt Morgan: There are some situations for a big man to come off the top rope. Undertaker does it. Kane does it. That's what sets them apart, in my opinion, from any other big man . . . is the fact that those two are the most athletically gifted big men I've seen. Those two are the reasons

Nick Bockwinkel, Verne Gagne, Bobby Heenan, and others on tour with the AWA

I'm wrestling, to be honest with you. Besides Andre and Big John Studd, definitely Taker and Kane. Big fans of them.

Nick Bockwinkel: I would say, I'd love to have a match with Kurt Angle. I'd like to have a match with Shawn Michaels. I'd like to have a match with any of the Guerreros. There are so many talents that, when I do turn on the wrestling and I watch it, there are so many that command my respect and command my admiration. God bless. I mean, the bumps these guys take today make it look like we were just big wimps. The chances they take today and, I mean, I remember one night — I think it was [Eddie] Guerrero and Kurt Angle — I'm sitting there watching the match and I'm screaming and yelling in the living room. My wife says, "What are you watching?" I said, "Wrestling." She says, "And it's got you going?" I said, "I'll talk to you later . . ." I mean, the match was just dynamic. . . .